December 1970

To Verl & Leona with
my best wishes.

Leon

JOSEPH SMITH: PROPHET of the Restoration

by

Leon R. Hartshorn

Published By
Deseret Book Company
Salt Lake City, Utah
1970

LITHOGRAPHED BY

IN THE UNITED STATES OF AMERICA

Preface

The physicians had ceased their efforts; nothing more could be done. Family members came close to pay their final respects. The venerable old prophet was dying. His eyes were closed; he was apparently unconscious. Suddenly he opened his eyes and in a strong voice uttered one word three times: "Joseph! Joseph! Joseph!" And then Brigham Young closed his eyes for the last time.

A young boy shines the shoes of an old patriarch and then inquires, "Please, sir. You knew Joseph Smith. Would you tell me about him?"

A timid Elder from a small town, new in the mission field, hears the words "You don't really believe that Joseph Smith story yourself!" and then the door abruptly closes. He walks down the path. Suddenly he stops, retraces his steps, and knocks at the door. Though frightened, he speaks boldly: "You said I didn't know Joseph Smith was a prophet of God. I want you to know that I know he is. I know he saw God the Father and His Son Jesus Christ. I know he translated the Book of Mormon."

Almost half-way around the world, another young man is confronted by one who has a superior education. The young man does not have the knowledge or the training to meet the arguments. Suddenly the young man stands up, looks directly into the eyes of the man with the fine education, grips him by the shoulders, and says: "I haven't had much education. My father died when I was fourteen, and I've been running a ranch to help support my mother and brothers and sisters. But I know that Joseph Smith is a Prophet of God!"

What a lasting impact this latter-day Joseph has had upon the lives of a large segment of mankind!

What manner of man was this Joseph Smith?

CONTENTS

1 UNCOMMON COURAGE

Twins: A Boy and a Girl

The year was 1832. Joseph Smith was living in Hiram, Ohio. Although he was a prophet, he was not insulated from nor isolated from hardship, suffering, or sorrow. In the year 1828, Emma Smith had given birth to a child while she and the Prophet were living in Harmony, Pennsylvania. The child, a son, died the same day. In 1831, a year prior to our 1832 setting, Emma had given birth to twins—a boy and a girl. What joy there must have been in the Smith household that day, but how shortlived was that joy. Before the sun had set, both infants were dead. Strangely enough, on that very same day, Sister John Murdock, who lived nearby, also gave birth to twins; and they also were a boy and a girl. The twins lived, but Sister Murdock died. Can you picture in your mind the Prophet—a young man, a large man, a sorrowing man—visiting with John Murdock? They exchanged sympathetic expressions. If you have never read the story, you can guess the outcome. When John Murdock's twins were nine days old, they were brought to Emma—a boy and a girl. These babies, adopted by the Prophet and his wife, would in a measure replace those buried. These babies would ease Emma Smith's aching heart.[1]

---

[1]Smith, Joseph, *History of the Church of Jesus Christ of Latter-day Saints* (Salt Lake City: Deseret News Press, 1948), 1:260. Hereafter abbreviated HC.

Preached a Sermon and Baptized Three

That same year, John Johnson, a successful farmer from Hiram, a small community located a short distance from Kirtland, came to that community to meet the Prophet Joseph Smith and to hear the message of the restored gospel. Before the meeting, John Johnson asked the Prophet if the gospel he espoused included miracles. The Prophet assured him that it did. It is probable that Joseph knew what prompted the question. Sister Johnson, standing at the side of her husband, had had a useless arm for many years. Joseph Smith preached the word of the Lord to those assembled; and then, apparently without warning, he crossed the room, took Mrs. Johnson's hand in his own and said, "In the Name of Jesus Christ I command thee to be made whole."[2]

Shortly afterward, John Johnson invited the Prophet and his family to come to live with him in his spacious farm house at Hiram. The Prophet gladly accepted the invitation. At the time he was engaged in revising the Bible, and this assistance was most welcome.

The Prophet's children were subject to illness as were other children; and in March, 1832, both of the infants had the measles. This necessitated not just one but both parents' being up with the babies for several nights. Finally, near midnight one night, the Prophet insisted that his wife go into an adjoining room to get some rest. She was reluctant, but he was persistent. He assured her that he would listen for any outcry from their little son, who was the sicker of the two infants. She consented and retired to the next room. Joseph lay down on a small bed next to the crib of the little boy Joseph. He had intended to listen, but soon fatigue overcame him, and he was asleep.

Unknown to him, a mob of some forty men had gathered in the woods a short distance from the house, where they waited patiently for the lamps to be extinguished. After the house became dark, they continued to wait until they were certain that all of its occupants were asleep. They approached

[2]HC, p. 216.

quietly and opened the door, and the Prophet, sleeping very soundly, was in their grasp and raised from his bed before the screams of his wife, Emma, awoke him. He fought desperately to free himself. He was an athletic man, powerfully built, six feet tall and weighing over 200 pounds. He managed to free one leg and kicked one of the mobsters with tremendous force. The mobster reeled back, landed on the frozen earth, and cried out, in essence, "Don't let loose of him, don't let loose of him. If you let loose of him, he'll run over the lot of us." He then choked the Prophet Joseph. The Prophet was carried several hundred feet from the house. His clothing was torn from him, and the mob tried to force acid into his mouth. He clenched his teeth and resisted. They cursed him and slammed the bottle against his teeth until they chipped one of his front teeth and spilled the acid on the ground. As they called for the bucket of tar, one of the mobsters was so filled with hate that he could not contain himself, and he fell upon the unprotected body of Joseph Smith and said, "G-- D--- you, I'll show you how the Holy Ghost falls on a person." He then began to scratch the flesh of the Prophet. Joseph Smith was then covered with the hot tar and left on the ground.[3]

Eventually, he partially recovered his strength and started toward the house. In the meantime Emma had gathered up her sick babies and taken them out into the cold night to hide them, fearing the mob would return and do them harm. She returned to the house before Joseph did and was there to open the door when he called to her. As she looked upon her husband covered with tar and blood, she thought that he was completely covered with blood. The shock was more than she could stand, and she fainted. Joseph called out again, and Brother Johnson appeared with a blanket. Joseph wrapped it around himself and went into the house. The remainder of the night was spent removing the tar. The washing and scraping was done under the direction of Dr. Fredrick G. Williams, with others assisting.

---

[3]*Ibid.*, pp. 261-64.

At this point, Joseph Smith had an opportunity to exercise his moral free agency. He had little choice in the events of the evening, but he had complete choice in how he would react to that which had happened to him. He could gather a large group of men and abuse those who abused him. He could curse those who have injured him. He could lie in bed and feel sorry for himself, he could question God, or he could select a more noble kind of behavior. The next paragraph in the writings of the Prophet reveals not only the behavior that the Prophet selected, but also gives us tremendous insight into his nature. Joseph recorded the events of the night in a concise, objective, factual way. Then he said that with the rising of the sun it was the Sabbath day, and he records very simply, "I preached a sermon and baptised three."[4] That is the end of the account. Some serve the Lord Jesus Christ when it is convenient; some serve when it is inconvenient. Joseph Smith served his Lord even when it was most inconvenient.

Five days later, one of the twins, the little boy, died, very possibly from the exposure to the cold night air.[5] Many will read the story of Joseph and his wife Emma laying the little body of Joseph in a small grave and think to themselves, "The Murdock baby died." Others, including parents of adopted children, will consider the account and will say, "Joseph and Emma lost a son, a son they had named Joseph." They would know that a child, adopted or natural, shares exactly the same place in a parent's heart. Joseph and Emma Smith's hearts were breaking that March day in 1832, as they laid their tiny son to rest.

The Prophet Joseph Smith displayed great physical courage while being abused by the mob. However, the Prophet displayed an even greater kind of courage. Let's go back to that spring of 1820 in New York.

Joseph Smith Knew and Would Always Know

Young Joseph Smith walked slowly, thoughtfully, toward

[4]*Ibid.*
[5]*Ibid.*, p. 265.

a grove of trees a short distance from the farm house where he resided in western New York State. For three years he had been searching to find the truth. In that period of time he had talked to many religionists but had received no satisfactory answers. He had come to realize after reading James 1:5—"If any of you lack wisdom, let him ask of God, that giveth to all men liberally, and upbraideth not; and it shall be given him"— that the only place he could obtain his answer was from God. He made up his mind to approach the Lord.

Perhaps he hesitated momentarily as he reached the grove, to determine if he was alone, since this was his first attempt at praying vocally. As he prayed, he was literally attacked by an unseen power that nearly destroyed him. Then a brilliant light began to appear, and that light dispelled the darkness that had bound him. In the light's midst were two glorious heavenly beings. Joseph Smith, not yet fifteen years of age, was privileged to communicate with God the Father and his Son Jesus Christ. He was told that he must join none of the churches and that he should wait for further word from the Lord. The remarkable vision closed, and when he regained his strength he returned to the house.[6]

There would be those who would question his story and those who would totally reject it, and there would be others who would rebuke and persecute him. But he knew, and would always know, that he had seen a vision. How can one feel the power of darkness, and then behold in mid-day a light brighter than the sun, and see and hear and talk with two heavenly beings—the Father and the Son—and wonder if something unusual has happened? There were those who would never know, but Joseph Smith knew and would always know that he had, that day, beheld a remarkable vision.

A Fateful Meeting

Nearly three and one-half years elapsed, and Joseph had received no further manifestations. In the evening of September 21, 1823, Joseph Smith retired to his bedroom and knelt in

---

[6]Pearl of Great Price, Writings of Joseph Smith 2:11-25. Hereafter abbreviated JS.

prayer. He prayed and prayed and prayed. He said he didn't know how long he prayed, but all noise in the house had ceased. All had long since gone to sleep, and yet he continued in prayer. He supposed that it must have been midnight, or perhaps later, and still he prayed.

Suddenly the entire room was filled with light which was truly like lightning, except that it was more pure and refined. Joseph said that it caused him to lose strength in the extremities of his body; but immediately afterwards, a feeling of warmth and peace filled his being, and he was not afraid. Standing before him in a pillar of light was a glorious heavenly being, and Joseph Smith records that although the entire room was filled with light above the brightness of the sun, the light in the room was not nearly as bright as the light which surrounded the personage who stood before him.[7] The heavenly visitor spoke and introduced himself as Moroni, an ancient inhabitant of the American continent. He told Joseph Smith of an ancient book which could bring eternal life. What a fateful meeting that September, 1823.

Moroni was his own best witness of the truthfulness of the message he was to deliver. He was an ancient prophet, a military leader, an author, a keeper of the sacred records, the last survivor of his nation, and one who had evaded his enemies year after year. He stood before young Joseph Smith as a glorious being who had just come from the presence of God. Moroni's very appearance bore eloquent testimony of his message. And then there was Joseph Smith, one whose birth had been announced by an ancient prophet, one who while yet of tender years had beheld the Father and the Son in the greatest vision ever given to man. Moroni had lived his earth life and was a proven valiant servant of God. Joseph Smith was just beginning his mission on earth, but his potential was astonishing. Yes, it was a fateful meeting. A meeting of such importance that it would be recalled and retold over and over by millions.

---

[7]Francis W. Kirkham, *A New Witness for Christ in America* (Salt Lake City: Brigham Young University, 1960), p. 86.

Joseph describes Moroni's appearance as follows:

He had on a loose robe of most exquisite whiteness. It was a whiteness beyond anything earthly I had ever seen; nor do I believe that any earthly thing could be made to appear so exceedingly white and brilliant. His hands were naked, and his arms also, a little above the wrist; so, also, were his feet naked, as were his legs, a little above the ankles. His head and neck were also bare. . . . Not only was his robe exceedingly white, but his whole person was glorious beyond description. . . .[8]

Joseph noted some additional interesting details. He described Moroni as being a little above the size of the average man of the day, and also, interestingly enough, said that Moroni's robe was apparently without seam—"without seam"—Joseph noted that detail.[9]

Moroni told Joseph that there was a book deposited, written upon gold plates, giving an account of the former inhabitants of this continent and the source from whence they sprang. He also said that the fulness of the everlasting gospel was contained in it, as delivered by the Savior to the ancient inhabitants.[10]

After the heavenly messenger had delivered his message, all of the light in the room gathered immediately into Moroni (a very brilliant angel in a very dark room), and a conduit of light opened above his head. He ascended and disappeared, and the entire room was dark. As Joseph pondered the remarkable manifestation and those things revealed to him, without warning the room was again filled with brilliant light, and the same messenger ascended. He did not say, "I have something additional to tell you," or "I want to emphasize," or "I forgot something." He just repeated all that he had said before, just as if he had never been there. Then, as before, the light gathered into the heavenly messenger and he ascended through the conduit of light; and again all was dark. You can imagine Joseph's surprise when the entire proceeding was repeated once again without warning or explanation. The angel told Joseph

[8]JS 2:31-32.
[9]Kirkham, p. 87.
[10]JS 2:34.

that his sins were forgiven and that his name would be had for good and evil and that he should tell his father all that had happened. After the third visit by the angel it was morning. The visits had consumed nearly the entire night.

Jesus taught persistence in prayer.[11] I have often wondered what the outcome would have been if Joseph had only prayed five minutes, or fifteen minutes, or if he had prayed for an hour or two hours. If he had not prayed as long as he did, he would, I assume, have gone to bed and thought, "I wonder why God won't answer my prayer." I am grateful Joseph Smith persisted.

The Good and the Evil

Joseph arose to go to the field to work as usual. He was obviously tired. He had had little sleep, and he had an intense spiritual experience. Joseph was exhausted; and his father, seeing that his son did not appear to be well, sent him to the house. As he climbed the rail fence which surrounded the field, he fell; and the same messenger appeared again and related all that had been said the previous night, and also, according to the Prophet's mother said, "Why did you not tell your father that which I had commanded you to tell him?" Joseph replied, "I was afraid my father would not believe me."[12]

Joseph Smith was seventeen years old. It would be somewhat hard for a young man of that age to approach his father and say, "Do you know what happened to me last night? An angel surrounded by light appeared three times and told me about golden plates buried," etc.

The hesitancy is understandable, but Joseph Smith was instructed to tell his father without delay, which he did; and his father assured him it was of God and that he should do all the angel had instructed him to do. The previous night he had seen the hill and the repository of the plates in vision. Now he walked to the hill, obtained a pole to use as a lever, and pried off the stone which was covering the cement box

---

[11]See Luke 11:1-13; 18:1-5.
[12]Smith, Lucy Mack, *History of Joseph Smith* (Salt Lake City: Bookcraft, 1958), p. 79. Hereafter abbreviated HJS.

containing the ancient records. He reached out to take the plates, and as he did so, he thought of the great value of the contents of the box. As he touched the plates, he was shocked. He tried again and was shocked again, and the shock was greater than the first one. Undaunted, he tried a third time, and this time the shock was so great that it deprived him of his natural strength; and he was afraid to try again to remove the plates. He cried out, "Why can I not obtain this book?" I do not think he expected an answer, but he received one. The ancient guardian of the plates stood before him and said, "Because you have not kept the commandments of the Lord."[13] He had not remembered the instruction of the previous night. Joseph sought God's forgiveness, and soon "his mind and soul were enlightened as they had been the night before, and he was filled with the Holy Spirit." The heavens were opened, and the glory of the Lord shone around about and rested upon him. As he gazed, enthralled, Moroni directed his attention to another vision by saying, "Look." And as Joseph turned, he was shown a vision of Satan and his followers. He was permitted to see the great contrast between the power of God and the power of Satan, and then the angel said:

All this is shown, the good and the evil, the holy and the impure, the glory of God and the power of darkness, that ye may know hereafter the two powers and never be influenced or overcome by that wicked one. Behold, whatever entices and leads to good and to do good, is of God, and whatever does not is of what wicked one: it is he that fills the hearts of men with evil to walk in darkness and blaspheme God; and you may learn from henceforth, that his ways are to destruction, but the way of holiness is peace and rest . . . You have now beheld the power of God manifested and the power of Satan; you see that there is nothing that is desirable in the work of darkness; that they cannot bring happiness: that those who are overcome herewith are miserable, while on the other hand the righteous are blessed with a place in the kingdom of God where joy unspeakable surrounds them . . .[14]

---

[13]Kirkham, pp. 97-98.
[14]*Ibid.*, pp. 99-100.

What a startling lesson—a lesson which never diminished in vividness during the life of Joseph Smith.

Joseph's mother recalled this event and said of it:

The angel showed him, by contrast, the difference between good and evil, and likewise the consequences of both obedience and disobedience to the commandments of God, in such a striking manner, that the impression was always vivid in his memory until the very end of his days; and in giving a relation of this circumstance, not long prior to his death, he remarked, that ever afterwards he was willing to keep the commandments of God.[15]

In less than 24 hours, Joseph Smith had seen the angel Moroni five times, and each time he had spoken to him at length. He had seen the ancient gold plates, and had seen the glory of the heavens and had also seen Satan and his associates.

Joseph Was the One—the Only One

As Joseph walked away from the hill, *do you think there was any question in his mind that he had had some remarkable experiences?* Do you think he doubted the reality of the angel, the ancient Book of Mormon record, the reality of God or Satan? He would be ridiculed, mocked, threatened, but this would not change the reality of the events. Joseph knew—he knew that he knew. The world would try to make him believe otherwise. Perhaps at this early time the die was already cast. Perhaps even this early in his life there were only two alternatives. Either Joseph Smith would have to deny what he saw and heard, or he would have to give his life for what he saw and heard.

Joseph Smith was to meet the heavenly messenger once each year for four years on the same date to receive instructions and to be prepared for his task of translating the Book of Mormon. On September 22, 1827, Joseph Smith received the golden plates from their guardian, Moroni. Many times Joseph Smith had been warned to be alert and protect the valuable plates from evil men. Joseph, therefore, fearful that he had been under surveillance, carefully deposited the plates

---

[15]HJS, p. 81.

in a hollow birch log in the woods before returning home. The next day Joseph went to a neighboring town to work. His mother sent for him, informing him that people in the area were plotting to get the plates. Joseph Smith returned to the woods and obtained the plates from their hiding place. On his way home, he was attacked three times. He was a strong man and needed all of his strength to overpower his attackers. So exhausted was he that he had to lie down and rest in the front yard before he could continue into the house.[16]

Let us consider for a moment the interesting but difficult situation of Joseph Smith. He had seen the Father and the Son. He had seen the angel, not once, but many times. He had seen the glory of God and a vision of Satan on the hill; and he had the plates. But, he was the only one. No one else had seen the Father, the Son, a heavenly messenger, or Satan. He was alone—completely alone. It was not hard to imagine a conversation that may have gone something like this:

"Joseph, I believed you when you said you saw the Father, the Son, the angel; and now I believe you when you say you have the plates. You do have the plates, don't you?"

"Yes, I have them in a wooden chest in my room."

"May I see them?"

"No."

"Why not? I've supported you, believed you, helped you; why can't I see them?"

"Because the angel said I can't show them to anyone."

It's easy to see, is it not, how this sounded. How difficult the situation of Joseph was—how easy to ridicule his claims. Perhaps more than once the Smiths were greeted with: "Have there been any angels flying low over the Smith home lately?" And then there were bitterness, threats, and violence.

The Prophet's brother Alvin had passed away before Joseph Smith had received the plates. He was a great soul and had totally supported his younger brother, Joseph, as indicated by the following comment by Joseph's mother:

---

[16]*Ibid.*, pp. 107-8.

Alvin manifested, if such could be the case, greater zeal and anxiety in regard to the Record that had been shown to Joseph, than any of the rest of the family; in consequence of which we could not bear to hear anything said upon the subject. Whenever Joseph spoke of the Record, it would immediately bring Alvin to our minds, with all his zeal, and with all his kindness; and, when we looked to his place, and realized that he was gone from it, to return no more in this life, we all with one accord wept over our irretrievable loss, and we could not be comforted, because he was not.[17]

Events after the death of Alvin illustrate well the intensity of the persecution that had come upon the Smith family. Rumors were circulating around the area that Alvin's body had been dug up and desecrated. This was apparently so disturbing to the family that Joseph's father, Joseph Smith Sr., felt he must do something about it. The account of what he did was published in the form of a public statement in the local newspaper on September 25, 1824.

TO THE PUBLIC:

Whereas reports have been industriously put in circulation, that my son, Alvin, had been removed from the place of his interment and dissected; which reports every person possessed of human sensibility must know, are peculiarly calculated to harrow up the mind of a parent and deeply wound the feelings of relations—therefore, for the purpose of ascertaining the truth of such reports, I, with some of my neighbors this morning, repaired to the grave, and removing the earth, found the body which had not been disturbed. This method is taken for the purpose of satisfying the minds of those who may have heard the report, and of informing those who have put it in circulation, and that it is earnestly requested they would desist therefrom; and that it is believed by some that they have been stimulated more by desire to injure the reputation of certain persons that a philanthropy for the peace and welfare of myself and friends.

(Signed) Joseph Smith [Joseph Smith's Father][18]

How difficult it was for Joseph Smith to bear the burden! Joseph was the one—the only one—who had seen and heard, but never did he mention it. I like that quality in him—quiet courage and dignity, even at that early age.

---

[17] *Ibid.*, p. 89.

[18] Kirkham, p. 147. (Printed in the *Wayne Sentinel*, a weekly periodical of Palmyra, New York. The original papers are at the New York State Library, Albany, New York.)

A Burden Lifted

Finally a long-awaited day came. The translation was completed. Joseph Smith wanted those who cared for him to be present at the Whitmer farm in Fayette. His father was there, his mother, Oliver Cowdery, Martin Harris, and the Whitmers. He must have electrified the small group when he told them that this was the day when three others would behold the plates besides himself. He told Oliver Cowdery he would be one of the witnesses and David Whitmer would be another. And then, approaching Martin Harris, in essence he said, "Martin, you have got to humble yourself before God this day. If you do, you will also be privileged to be one of the witnesses."

The four left the house and went to the woods. They knelt and began to pray, praying vocally in turn. After each one had prayed twice, Martin Harris arose and said, "It is my fault that our prayers are not answered," and then he left. Shortly after his departure, a brilliant light appeared and an angel stood before them holding the plates and turning some of the leaves. They all heard the voice of God speak from the heavens, bearing witness that the translation was correct. As the vision closed, Joseph Smith went to find Martin Harris. He found him praying. He knelt with him, and they prayed together. The same vision was opened to them. They beheld an angel, saw the plates, and they heard the voice of God. Martin Harris was soon so overcome with joy that he cried out, " 'Tis enough. 'Tis enough. Mine eyes have beheld. Mine eyes have beheld."[19]

Joseph had been gone from the Whitmer home for a long time. As he entered the house, he did not speak. He sat down by his mother. He laid his head on his mother's breast. So much had happened to the young prophet in the past decade, though he was not yet twenty-four years old. He in essence said, quietly, reflectively: "Mother, you don't know what a burden has been lifted from me this day. Now people will know that I don't go around to deceive them. The Lord

---

[19]HC 1:54-55.

has caused that the plates have been shown to three others besides myself, and they must be witnesses with me."[20]

"You don't know what a burden has been lifted." Persecuted, hated, forced to move several times, and not one mention of it. How difficult it was until others shared it with him. Courage—call it moral, mental—but what courage! Joseph Smith demonstrated extreme courage the night he was abused and covered with hot tar, but the exercise of courage in the face of overwhelming opposition had become a characteristic of Joseph Smith long before that March evening in 1832.

---

[20]HJS, p. 152.

2 PORTRAIT OF A PROPHET

A Great Missionary

The majority of the residents of New York rejected young Joseph Smith as a brash upstart. There were a few, however, who believed and were excited with the opportunity to do God's will in this day and age and to receive instructions from him. The believing few approached the Prophet with a simple, humble, worthy request: "Joseph, would you please inquire of the Lord and see what he would like me to do; I would like to do the will of the Lord."

Those who came represented a rather diversified group. Some were relatively wealthy and some were poor; some were well educated by the standards of the day, and others were largely untutored; some were older, and some were not yet out of their teens. Yet the answer was always the same to all of these requests: "I say unto you, that the thing which will be of most worth unto you will be to . . . bring souls unto me."[1] And further: "And if it so be that you should labor all your days in crying repentance unto this people, and bring, save it be one soul unto me, how great shall be your joy with him in the kingdom of my Father!"[2] The message should not be surprising when we consider the value that the Lord has always placed upon the worth of a soul.

Joseph Smith was commanded by the Lord to take the

---

[1]Doctrine and Covenants of The Church of Jesus Christ of Latter-day Saints, 15:6. Hereafter referred to as D&C.
[2]D&C 18:15.

gospel to every nation, kindred, tongue, and people; and he immediately started out to do it. He was a missionary from the beginning. His first converts to the restored gospel were members of his own family. They believed that their son and brother was a youth of integrity; and when he spoke, he spoke the truth. Soon friends of the family and neighbors heard of the unusual experiences of Joseph Smith—they listened, they learned, they believed.

Joseph Smith sought for opportunities to preach and bear witness of the gospel, and he apparently had a great capacity to interest and inspire. Brigham Young said:

What a delight it was to hear brother Joseph talk upon the great principles of eternity; he would bring them down to the capacity of a child, and he would unite heaven with earth, this is the beauty of our religion.[3]

On another occasion, Brigham Young also referred to Joseph's remarkable ability as a teacher:

The excellency of the glory of the character of brother Joseph Smith was that he could reduce heavenly things to the understanding of the finite. When he preached to the people— revealed the things of God, the will of God, the plan of salvation, the purposes of Jehovah, the relation in which we stand to him and all the heavenly beings, he reduced his teachings to the capacity of every man, woman, and child, making them as plain as a well-defined pathway. This should have convinced every person that ever heard of him of his divine authority and power, for no other man was able to teach as he could, and no person can reveal the things of God, but by the revelations of Jesus Christ. When we hear a man that can speak of heavenly things, and present them to the people in a way that they can be understood, you may know that to that man the avenue is open, and that he, by some power, has communication with heavenly beings; and when the highest intelligence is exhibited, he, perhaps, has communication with the highest intelligence that exists.[4]

Daniel H. Wells was also impressed by the teaching of the Prophet. Brother Wells was not a member of the Church during Joseph Smith's life but later became a prominent Church leader. He recalled Joseph as follows:

[3]*Journal of Discourses* 4:54. Hereafter referred to as JD.
[4]*Ibid.*, 8:206.

I knew nothing at all about Joseph, except what I had heard from his enemies or read in the papers. . . . I was introduced to Joseph Smith. . . . He was a fine looking man . . . I soon learned that he knew more about religion and the things of God and eternity than any man I had ever heard talk. . . . I obtained them [principles of the gospel] from Joseph, and it seemed to me that he advanced principles that neither he nor any other man could have obtained except from the Source of all wisdom—the Lord himself.[5]

Elder Charles W. Penrose was impressed with the Prophet's ability to not only receive from God for himself, but to assist others in also obtaining knowledge from God:

For he [Joseph Smith] received blessings to a greater degree than are poured out commonly upon the children of men . . . his mind was enlightened far beyond the condition of his fellowmen, for God bestowed upon him at the proper time the gift of the Holy Ghost. . . . And Joseph Smith learned how to obtain that glorious and heavenly gift not only for himself but for others, and he was enabled to instruct the inhabitants of the earth how they could obtain it . . . how they could come to a knowledge of His existence through this heavenly gift, so that they might be guided in his ways and know that they were walking in his paths.[6]

The Prophet Joseph Smith never missed an opportunity to preach the gospel. He was almost continually a missionary. When he visited Washington, D. C., he told the president of the United States about the gospel. While in prison, he taught the gospel to the guards. He also went on many missions. Following are a few representative entries from the Prophet's Journal.

Thursday, 24.—At the house of Mr. Beman, in Colburn, whence we left for Waterford, where we spoke to a small congregation; thence to Mount Pleasant, and preached to a large congregation the same evening, when Freeman A. Nickerson and his wife declared their belief in the work, and offered themselves for baptism. Great excitement prevailed in every place we visited.

Saturday, 26.—Preached at Mount Pleasant; the people were very tender and inquiring.

Sunday, 27.—Preached to a large congregation at Mount Pleasant, after which I baptized twelve, and others were deeply

---

[5]*Ibid.*, 12:71-72.
[6]*Ibid.*, 23:348-49.

impressed, and desired another meeting, which I appointed for the day following.

Monday, 28.—In the evening, we broke bread, and laid on hands for the gift of the Holy Ghost, and for confirmation, having baptized two more. The Spirit was given in great power to some, and peace to others.

Tuesday, 29—After preaching at 10 o'clock a.m., I baptized two, and confirmed them at the water's side. Last evening we ordained F. A. Nickerson an Elder.[7]

Joseph Smith's unceasing efforts to bring people to the Lord resulted in the organization of several little branches in the same year the Church was organized. Those new converts experienced persecution just as their prophet had, but they felt joy in their hearts and hoped for a better life for themselves and for others.

A Dream of Zion—a Better Life

A little group of Saints and several candidates for baptism approached a stream of water which had been previously dammed so the water would be deep enough to perform the ordinance. They were dismayed to find that the dam had been removed. This was only one in a series of harassments. The services were of necessity postponed. The dam was replaced; and under cover of darkness, the new converts went into the water of baptism.[8] This incident took place in the latter part of the year 1830 in Colesville, New York.

The Saints were further harassed. On one occasion Joseph Smith was arrested after delivering a sermon to a gathering of the Saints. The sheriff, in reality, was in league with a group of individuals who disliked the Prophet Joseph intensely, and he (the sheriff) was to meet them outside of Colesville and deliver Joseph Smith into their hands. He was, however, so impressed with the Prophet after being in his presence just a few minutes that he realized that he had been deceived concerning the character of the man he had arrested. When they approached the mob, he whipped his horse and raced by

---

[7]HC 1:422.
[8]*Ibid.*, pp. 88-89.

them. They, stunned momentarily by the unexpected turn of events, then recovered and gave chase, shouting for the sheriff to stop. Because the mob was on foot, they were left in the distance. Just at that inopportune moment, however, a wheel came off the buggy. They retrieved the wheel, replaced it and secured it. The mob drew closer, shouting for the sheriff to stop. Just in time, the sheriff and his prisoner leaped into the wagon and outran their pursuers. When they arrived at an inn, the sheriff gave the Prophet the bed. He lay with his feet against the door, with his pistol in hand to assure the safety of the man whom just a few hours previously he had thought to be a despicable individual.[9]

The members of the Colesville branch were acquainted with persecution. They were also familiar with hunger, poverty, and suffering. They were not unacquainted with the teachings of the Book of Mormon. They had read in the book of the wonderful conditions among the early inhabitants of the continent after the visit of the Lord Jesus Christ to them. There was no contention in all the land, and the people could not have been happier. There were no dissensions among them, and they were blessed of God and prospered.[10]

Now the Prophet gave to them and others in 1830 some of the most remarkable revelations ever given to man; these were concerning Moses and Enoch. He taught that Enoch had established a holy city called ZION. In it there was an absence of sin, suffering, and poverty—and an abundance of joy. "And the Lord called his people ZION, because they were of one heart and one mind, and dwelt in righteousness; and there was no poor among them."[11] The Lord gave Enoch such strength that his people were miraculously protected from their enemies as Enoch moved mountains and changed the course of rivers and they came up no more against them. Then the entire city and all of its inhabitants were taken up into heaven.[12]

---

[9]*Ibid.*, pp. 88, 89.
[10]4 Nephi 10-18.
[11]Moses 7:18.
[12]Moses 7:13-23.

We can imagine how impressive this must have been to the little group of persecuted, beleaguered Colesville Saints. How excited they also must have been with an additional teaching of the Book of Mormon that in the latter days a Holy City (Zion) would be established on the American Continent.[13] Perhaps they asked Joseph Smith, "What about Zion for us? May we also, as God's people, have a righteous place and be protected from our enemies? Can we have a happy existence, where there is no poverty or suffering?"

In the latter part of 1831, the Lord said to Joseph Smith that it was His will that the Saints "assemble together at the Ohio."[14] The Lord had spoken, and the Prophet prepared for the move. When the Colesville Saints learned of the revelation, they sold their property and moved as a group to Ohio.

Joseph Smith's arrival in Kirtland was most interesting. Near the first of February, a sleigh containing four persons stopped in front of the Gilbert and Whitney store. Joseph got out of the sleigh and entered the store and said, "Newel K. Whitney! Thou art the man!" As he and the Prophet shook hands, Newel Whitney said, "You have the advantage of me. I could not call you by name as you have me." "I am Joseph, the Prophet. You've prayed me here, now what do you want of me?" Brother Whitney said, "So I have." He then invited Joseph and Emma to reside in an apartment above the store.[15]

Shortly after Joseph arrived in Ohio, the Lord revealed that twenty-eight elders, including the Prophet were to travel through the western country preaching the gospel and meet in a conference in Missouri. In obedience to the Lord, the Prophet set out on the nearly one thousand mile journey to Missouri. After he arrived, he petitioned the Lord to learn the exact location of Zion; and the Lord said that he was now in Zion, that the center place of Zion was Independence,

---

[13]Ether 13:3-6.
[14]D&C 37:3.
[15]HC 1:146.

Jackson County, Missouri.[16] Joseph Smith was delighted with
Zion and wrote:

> . . . As far as the eye can reach, the beautiful rolling prairies
> spread out like a sea of meadows; and are decorated with a growth
> of flowers so gorgeous and grand as to exceed description; and
> nothing is more fruitful or a richer stockholder in the blooming
> prairie then the honey bee. Only on the water courses is timber to
> be found. There, in strips from one to three miles in width, and
> following faithfully the meanderings of the streams, it grows in
> luxuriant forests. The forests are a mixture of oak, hickory, black
> walnut, elm, ash, cherry, honey locust, mulberry, coffee bean, hack-
> berry, box elder and basswood; with the addition of cottonwood,
> butterwood, pecan and soft and hard maple upon the bottoms. The
> shrubbery is beautiful and consists of plums, grapes, crab apples
> and persimmons.
> The soil is rich and fertile; from three to ten feet deep, and
> generally composed of a rich black mold, intermingled with clay
> and sand. It yields in abundance.[17]

Joseph Smith and his followers had a dream of Zion. Joseph
had sought to know the location of Zion, and after traveling
several hundred miles over a period of many weeks, he finally
received the answer. What a fascinating example of exercising
faith in the Lord Jesus Christ!

To the Edge of the Light

President David O. McKay told the following story in a
general conference in 1936. The story was repeated by Elder
Henry D. Moyle in 1956:

> There is a story that has oft been told by President McKay,
> particularly during the early days of the welfare program that I
> should like to repeat. It is the story of an engineer who pulled his
> train into a station one dark and stormy night, and while the engineer
> was going calmly about oiling his engine, getting ready for the
> next run, a timid passenger from the coach came up to him and asked
> him if he were not afraid of going out into the dark. Without
> looking up, the engineer said, "I'm not pulling my train out into
> the dark tonight." "Oh, I beg your pardon, I thought you were going

[16]Roberts, B. H., *A Comprehensive History of the Church of Jesus Christ of Latter-day Saints* (Salt Lake City: Deseret News Press, 1930), 1:254-55. Hereafter referred to as CHC
[17]HC 1:197.

to be our engineer," said the man. "I am, but I wouldn't be in the dark tonight." He said, "Why, I should think you would be very nervous with the lives of all these men and women on this train depending upon you." For an answer, the engineer pointed up to the headlight that threw an intense white light several hundred yards ahead on the track and said, "When I pull out and when I get there, that light will be extended several hundred yards ahead, and I shall run to the end of that light and so on throughout the night. I'll be running in the light all the way." And the man replied, "Thanks for the lesson, faithful engineer."

President McKay continued: "I can say this to you: The first circle of light we have seen is October 1, 1936, when by that date we shall see to it that we have sufficient food, fuel, clothing, etc., to see every needy family through this coming winter, and by the time we get to October 1st, the light will have extended sufficiently far to permit us to see the next move we should make. I can promise you one thing, that we'll be running in the light all the way through this dark night."[18]

What marvelous description of faith!

Run to the edge of the light. If we sat and waited until the light shone to the end of the road, we would wait a long time. Faith is going to the edge of the light.

Joseph Smith desired to know the location of Zion. The Lord said, go to Ohio; that was the edge of the light, and Joseph went to the edge of the light. He prayed again and was led to Missouri; again, he traveled to the edge of the light and ultimately received his answer. What a lesson in faith for all of us.

A Broken Dream

When the Colesville Saints learned that the centerplace, Zion, was in Missouri, they moved as a group to Missouri. The Lord had revealed a Zion location. He also revealed the physical plans for a Zion City, with wide streets and large lots. They were also to have a new kind of economy, a Zion economy, called the "law of consecration."

If ever a people had a dream, if ever a people had high expectations, it was the Latter-day Saints moving to Independence, Jackson County, Missouri in the year of 1831. They were

[18]*Conference Report*, April 1956, pp. 59, 60. Hereafter referred to as CR.

going to build a city where there would be no sin, no poverty, no injustice. They would build a city, a temple—a place for the Lord to dwell. They would prepare for the ushering in of the Millennium, a thousand years of peace.

How excited they were about Zion—no sickness, no evil, no poverty, no persecution. How great were their dreams. Never did a leader and a little band of followers have higher expectations.

After two years, disaster struck, and those who had gone to build the City of God had now been cruelly driven from their homes and were huddled north of the Missouri River enduring sleet and snow. Only hopes that had been built so high could be dashed so low. But still there was hope; the Lord had given them Zion. Joseph Smith gathered a group of faithful and fashioned them into an army of over 200 men and marched with them the 1,000 miles to Missouri—tortuous miles, miles punctuated with blistered feet and tired muscles and strained nerves. But it was worth the effort because the governor of Missouri had said that if he had sufficient assistance, he would reestablish the Mormons to their legally owned lands. He, however, when the opportunity arrived to be of help, did not keep his word, and the men, disappointed, returned to Kirtland. Many were even more loyal to the Prophet. Others were disenchanted with Joseph Smith and the restored gospel. The long journey extracted from them more than they could endure for any cause. Joseph Smith remained firm and immovable in his belief that the Saints would be reinstated in Jackson County.

The Saints relocated in several counties in northern Missouri. At Far West, Caldwell County, corner stones for a temple were laid. The old bitterness, however, continued. Saints were abused and driven from their homes, and Joseph told the Saints to gather at Far West for their mutual protection.

The Betrayal of the Prophet

Finally the destruction came at Far West, and the Prophet was betrayed into the hands of his enemies by Colonel George

Hinkle, a trusted associate. Joseph was one of the several Church leaders to be so betrayed. Parley Pratt wrote of that first abusive night when he, Joseph Smith, and others were prisoners:

> We were placed under a strong guard, and were without shelter during the night, lying on the ground in the open air, in the midst of a great rain. The guards during the whole night kept up a constant tirade of mockery, and the most obscene blackguardism and abuse. They blasphemed God; mocked Jesus Christ; swore the most dreadful oaths; taunted Brother Joseph and others; demanded miracles; wanted signs, such as "Come Mr. Smith, show us an angel." "Give us one of your revelations." "Show us a miracle." "Come, there is one of your brethren here in camp whom we took prisoner yesterday in his own house, and knocked his brains out with his own rifle, which we found hanging over his fireplace; he lays speechless and dying; speak the word and heal him, and then we will all believe." "Or, if you are Apostles or men of God, deliver yourselves, and then we will be Mormons." Next would be a volley of oaths and blasphemies; then a tumultuous tirade of lewd boastings of having defiled virgins and wives by force, etc., much of which I dare not write; and, indeed, language would fail me to attempt more than a faint description. Thus passed this dreadful night, and before morning several other captives were added to our number. . . .[19]

The Prophet's life was spared only by the courageous act of Alexander Doniphan. Brigadier General Doniphan received an illegal order from his commanding officer Major General Samuel D. Lucas to take Joseph Smith and the other prisoners into the public square at 9:00 the next morning and shoot them. General Doniphan wasted no time in sending the following bold reply to his superior officer:

> It is cold-blooded murder. I will not obey your order. My brigade shall march for Liberty tomorrow morning at 8:00; and if you execute these men, I will hold you responsible before an earthly tribunal, so help me God.
>
> (signed) A. W. Doniphan
> Brigadier General[20]

The Latter-day Saints were disarmed by the Missourians and were left defenseless before soldiers who, when dismissed,

---

[19]*Autobiography of Parley P. Pratt* (Salt Lake City: Deseret Book Co., 1966), p. 187.
[20]HC 3:190-91.

became a raging mob. Few were spared; the mob rode relentlessly through the streets of the Mormon city shooting animals, looting, beating the men, and raping the women and girls. As the prophet later reflected upon the brutality of their adversaries, he wrote:

> . . . The inhumanity and murderous disposition of this people! It shocks all nature; it beggars and defies all description; it is a tale of woe; a lamentable tale; yea a sorrowful tale; too much to tell; too much for contemplation; too much for human beings; it cannot be found among the heathens; it cannot be found among the nations where kings and tyrants are enthroned; it cannot be found among the savages of the wilderness; yea, and I think it cannot be found among the wild and ferocious beasts of the forest—that a man should be mangled for sport! Women be robbed of all that they have—their last morsel for subsistence, and then be violated to gratify the hellish desires of the mob, and finally left to perish with their helpless offspring clinging around their necks. . . .[21]

The prisoners were to be taken southward to Jackson County to be imprisoned. Prior to their departure, they were premitted a brief visit to see their families. Joseph records:

> . . . We were led into the public square, and after considerable entreaty, we were permitted to see our families, being attended by a strong guard. I found my family in tears . . . they clung to my garments weeping. I requested to have a private interview with my wife in an adjoining room, but was refused; when taking my departure from my family, it was almost too painful for me. My children clung to me, and were thrust away at the point of the swords of the soldiery. . . .[22]

The prisoners were placed in a wagon, and a jeering mob gathered around them. The parents of Joseph and Hyrum made their way through the crowd and grasped the hands of their captive sons. They were not permitted to speak. The Prophet, his brother Hyrum, and others were displayed in various communities and imprisoned temporarily at Richmond, Missouri. The Prophet records that they had to sleep on the floor with only a mantle for their covering and a stick of wood for their pillows. The Prophet also commented on the food: "Our

---

[21]*Ibid.*, pp. 290-91.
[22]*Ibid.*, p. 371.

victuals were of the coarest kind, and served up in a manner which was disgusting."[23]

The Prophet's Anguish

The conditions were almost unbearable, and the poignant messages that the Prophet received from his friends telling of the things they had to endure, combined with wicked, obscene boasts of his captors, brought anguish to his soul. He reflected upon the injustices which were taking place as the saints were being driven from the state in cold weather. The hours slowly passed, and then a change of the guard. They arrived boasting loudly of new deeds of robbery, rape, and murder. The Prophet Joseph listened, as he had countless times before, to that which had and was taking place outside the prison. The vile harangue continued into the night. Finally Joseph could endure it no longer. Following is Parley Pratt's vivid description of what followed.

In one of those tedious nights we had lain as if in sleep till the hour of midnight had passed, and our ears and hearts had been pained, while we had listened for hours to the obscene jests, the horrid oaths, the dreadful blasphemies and filthy language of our guards . . . as they recounted to each other their deeds of rapine, murder, robbery, etc., which they had committed among the "*Mormons*" while at Far West and vicinity. They even boasted of defiling by force wives, daughters, and virgins, and of shooting or dashing out the brains of men, women and children.

I had listened till I became so disgusted, shocked, horrified, and so filled with the spirit of indignant justice, that I could scarcely refrain from rising upon my feet and rebuking the guards; but had said nothing to Joseph, or anyone else, although I lay next to him and knew he was awake. On a sudden he arose to his feet, and spoke in a voice of thunder, or as the roaring lion, uttering, as near as I can recollect, the following words:

"*SILENCE, ye fiends of the infernal pit. In the name of Jesus Christ I rebuke you, and command you to be still. I will not live another minute and hear such language. Cease such talk, or you or I die THIS INSTANT!*"

He ceased to speak. He stood erect in terrible majesty. Chained,

---

[23]*Ibid.*, pp. 371-73.

and without a weapon; calm, unruffled and dignified as an angel, he looked down upon the quailing guards . . . whose knees smote together, and who, shrinking into a corner, or crouching at his feet, begged his pardon, and remained quiet till a change of guards.

I have seen ministers of justice, clothed in magisterial robes, and criminals arraigned before them, while life was suspended upon a breath in the courts of England; I have witnessed a Congress in solemn session to give laws to nations; I have tried to conceive of kings, of royal courts, of thrones and crowns; and of emperors assembled to decide the fate of kingdoms; but dignity and majesty have I seen but once, as it stood in chains, at midnight, in a dungeon in an obscure village of Missouri.[24]

Let us remember that the anguished man in jail was Joseph Smith. Not yet 33 years of age, he was a prophet of God and he was the president of the Church of the Lord and Savior of the world, Jesus Christ.

Joseph Smith was by nature an active man. His knowledge of the importance of man's probationary period called "earth life" equaled or surpassed the knowledge of any man, except Jesus, who had ever lived on this earth. He had beheld Satan, outer darkness, and had seen this vividly contrasted with God and the celestial kingdom. He had seen the pre-existant life and knew of the destruction that would come upon the world if the people did not repent. He knew of the beautiful reality of the one-thousand-year reign of the Lord Jesus Christ upon the earth and that those who qualified would be with their Lord. He knew of impending war and death and destruction that would come upon the United States unless repentance came and changes were made.[25] With this kind of knowledge, combined with sensitivity and love, we can perhaps gain some insight into the fantastic motivation which Joseph had. He threw himself relentlessly into his task. He attacked the problems of sin, of evil, and sought to establish peace and salvation for all people of the world. Fortunately, Joseph Smith, not by accident, possessed a superior physical body and had great physical strength and endurance. This permitted him to carry out his ambitious desires—to curb wrong and establish right.

[24]*Pratt*, pp. 210-11.
[25]D&C 87.

Now let us consider for a moment what it must have been like for this rightly, highly motivated prophet to remain confined day after day, week after week, month after month in a small cell—confined for no just or reasonable cause. He was innocent, with a burning desire to do good, to teach, direct, bring principles of salvation, build the kingdom of God, and prepare the earth for the millennial reign—and with the setting of the sun each night felt the sheer frustration of senseless restraint brought by another day of confinement. How does one adapt to it month after month? This added to the obvious concern for his homeless, suffering followers, and the foul conditions of the prison were almost too much for the young prophet of the Lord.

The Prophet's Lament

The Prophet's longest imprisonment was in Liberty, Missouri. The Liberty Jail, an unlikely place with an unlikely name, was a small stone jail divided into two rooms. The cellar room was 14' x 14½' and the ceiling was 6½' high. The upper room was of the same dimensions, except that the ceiling was slightly higher.[26]

It is in the Liberty Jail that we have a remarkable opportunity to examine what the Prophet Joseph Smith is really like. We view a distressed prophet, still young. We view a prophet who feels anguish because of the poor, and much-injured Saints.

Joseph Smith had experienced life, not always good, sometimes bad; not always pleasant, sometimes painful; not always successful, sometimes unsuccessful. He had moved from Palmyra to Harmony, from Harmony to Fayette, to escape the bitter persecution. He had a dream of Zion and pursued that dream. He tried to establish a holy city in Jackson County, a city based upon the new economic principle, the law of consecration. He observed the Saints being driven from Jackson County. He envisioned a financial institution, the Kirtland Safety Society, which would bring security to the Saints. He saw

[26]N. B. Lundwall, *The Fate of the Persecuters of the Prophet Joseph Smith*, (Salt Lake City: Publisher's Press, 1952), p. 107.

the collapse of the Society and felt the wrath of some of those who were hurt by the failure. He hoped for a place of refuge for the Saints in Northern Missouri. He experienced the dashing of that hope. In my opinion, this was a climactic disappointment in a series of disappointments. The defeat at Far West was a crushing one. Joseph Smith was imprisoned, his Saints were turned out of their homes, hellish fury was unleashed. The result was great hardship, and this was almost more than the great soul of the Prophet Joseph Smith could bear. He reacted as a man—as a good man—but as a man. The first epistles from the Liberty Jail reflected this. He condemned the injustices. He named and condemned the apostates. He was indignant, and the tenor of his letters was injustice and the need for justice. Conditions did not improve. December passed and imprisonment continued. The harshness of February came, and still the crimes continued—still suffering, still death, still overwhelming injustice. The Prophet continued to ponder; and finally in March, it seems as though he was almost beside himself with grief because of the sufferings, the intense sufferings, of the much-injured Saints. He cried out in anguish to God:

O God, where art thou? And where is the pavilion that covereth thy hiding place?

How long shall thy hand be stayed, and thine eye, yea thy pure eye, behold from the eternal heavens the wrongs of thy people and of thy servants, and thine ear be penetrated with their cries?

Yea, O Lord, how long shall they suffer these wrongs and unlawful oppressions, before thine heart shall be softened toward them, and thy bowels be moved with compassion toward them.[27]

The Return of Hope

Even with this anguished cry to God, the answer was not forthcoming. The Prophet Joseph Smith's mind was filled with the events of the present and distressing thoughts of the future and fears of what it might hold. It is interesting that that which needed to go into his mind, which would act as a catalyst, came apparently from three letters—one from his wife, Emma;

---

[27]D&C 121:1-3.

one from his brother, Don Carlos; and one from his friend Edward Partridge. The Prophet Joseph Smith read and reread these letters filled with love, kindness, and hope; and then the Prophet said:

. . . We received some letters last evening—one from Emma, one from Don C. Smith, and one from Bishop Partridge—all breathing a kind and consoling spirit. We were much gratified with their contents. We had been a long time without information; and when we read those letters they were to our soul as the gentle air is refreshing, but our joy was mingled with grief, because of the sufferings of the poor and much injured Saints. And we need not say to you that the floodgates of our hearts were lifted and our eyes were a fountain of tears, but those who have not been enclosed in the walls of prison without cause or provocation, can have but little idea how sweet the voice of a friend is; one token of friendship from any source whatever awakens and calls into action every sympathetic feeling; it brings up in an instant everything that has passed; it seizes the present with the avidity of lightening; it grasps after the future with the fierceness of a tiger; it moves the mind backward and forward, from one thing to another, until finally all enmity, malice and hatred, and past differences misunderstandings and mismanagements are slain victorious at the feet of hope. . . .[28]

His mind moved forward and backward with the intensity, and finally "all enmity, malice, and hatred and past differences, misunderstandings, mismanagements are slain victorious at the feet of hope." Joseph continues:

When the heart is sufficiently contrite, the voice of the spirit steals along and whispers:

My son, peace be unto thy soul; thine adversity and thine afflictions shall be but a small moment;

And then, if thou endure it well, God shall exalt thee on high; thou shalt triumph over all thy foes.

Thy friends do stand by thee, and they shall hail thee again with warm hearts and friendly hands.

Thou art not yet as Job: thy friends do not contend against thee, neither charge thee with transgression, as they did Job.[29]

In his persecution, his anguish, his torment, he reached out to God. He had reached out ever so many times before. The

---

[28]HC 3:293.
[29]D&C 121:7-10.

Lord spoke not in the manner which Joseph Smith pleaded for—not in the way that he had initially wanted, an awesome display of power; he had wanted God's wrath to be shown. He had wanted vengence upon the wicked. One can petition God, but one cannot dictate to God. One cannot direct God. Yes, the Lord answered after Joseph Smith had fulfilled the law upon which the answer and the blessing were predicated. But the Lord characteristically selected when and how he would answer. He would not answer with a voice of thunder, but with a small voice, a whisper. He did not answer with destruction upon the heads of the wicked, but he answered with "peace be unto you." He did not destroy the enemies of Joseph Smith, but whispered tolerance, understanding, love, and hope to the heart of the Prophet. Yes, Jesus Christ had experienced suffering in the flesh so that he could succor his people; and the wise, gentle Jesus whispered hope and peace to the heart of a much maligned servant. With that message of hope and peace, and with the power, the gentle, loving power of God in his being, Joseph Smith emerged from disappointment and darkness into hope and light—what a transformation it was. It is remarkable to behold how Joseph Smith acted with courage, resolution, hope, love, and strength. It should encourage all who are disappointed and frustrated by the events of life to, in like manner, turn to Him who has all power and infinite love.

Joseph had relearned a sacred truth that the Lord requires of all, even a prophet, a "broken heart and contrite spirit."

In the Book of Mormon, the Lord instructed *all* of his followers that at his resurrection animal sacrifice was done away with, but he would now require a new sacrifice, the sacrifice of a "broken heart and a contrite spirit."[30] Assisted by reading those kind, loving, encouraging letters, the Prophet Joseph Smith became mentally and spiritually receptive to the promptings of the Holy Ghost; and there was a marvelous transformation in him. In my opinion, prior to this moment, Joseph Smith had been acting like a man, he had been reacting to his circumstances in a reasonable way, a just way and an

---

[30]3 Nephi 9:19-20.

expected way; but he had been reacting like a man—a good man, a great man—but a *man*. Now as we read the account we see, as so many times before, the Prophet Joseph Smith emerging. And what a transformation takes place as the Lord Jesus Christ, so well qualified, with all of the necessary credentials to stand at the head of the Church, inspires the Prophet Joseph Smith.

Joseph Smith Spoke with Power and Authority

Joseph spoke out with remarkable power. No more was he pleading and lamenting about the past, but he was now looking to the future; and he declared that nothing will stop the work of God. The kingdom will roll forth and fill the whole earth; and even if earth and hell combine against the Church, the Church will stand.

. . . Hell may pour forth its rage like the burning lava of mount Vesuvius, or of Etna, or of the most terrible of the burning mountains; and yet shall "Mormonism" stand. Water, fire, truth and God are all realities. Truth is "Mormonism." God is the author of it. He is our shield. It is by Him we received our birth. It was by His voice that we were called to a dispensation of His Gospel in the beginning of the fulness of times. It was by Him we received the Book of Mormon; and it is by Him that we remain unto this day; and by Him we shall remain, if it shall be for our glory; and in His Almighty name we are determined to endure tribulation as good soldiers unto the end. . . .[31]

The Prophet Joseph Smith wrote that three things are responsible for the hellish conditions that he and his people were suffering:

. . . But I bed leave to say unto you, brethren, that *ignorance, superstition* and *bigotry* placing itself where it ought not, is oftentimes in the way of the prosperity of this Church; like the torrent of rain from the mountains, that floods the most pure and crystal stream with mire, and dirt, and filthiness, and obscures everything that was clear before, and all rushes along in one general deluge; but time weathers tide; and notwithstanding we are rolled in the mire of the flood for the time being, the next surge peradventure, as time rolls on, may bring to us the fountain as clear as crystal, and

---

[31]HC 3:297.

as pure as snow, while the filthiness, floodwood and rubbish is left and purged out by the way. . . .[32] (Italics added.)

I do not think it would be fair to say that all of the ignorance, superstition, and bigotry was outside of the Church. The Lord, on occasion, had to rebuke the Latter-day Saints. Joseph compared the Church to a muddy stream but envisioned a day when ignorance, superstition, and bigotry would be done away with and the stream would be crystal clear. He then wrote this famous scripture:

How long can rolling waters remain impure? What power shall stay the heavens? As well might man stretch forth his puny arm to stop the Missouri river in its decreed course, or to turn it up stream, as to hinder the Almighty from pouring down knowledge from heaven upon the heads of the Latter-day Saints.[33]

Joseph continued his remarkable epistle with a strong admonition for the Saints to treat others in a way that they have not been treated.

Our religion is between us and our God. Their religion is between them and their God.

. . . There is a love from God that should be exercised toward those of our faith, who walk uprightly, which is peculiar to itself, but it is without prejudice; it also gives scope to the mind, which enables us to conduct ourselves with greater liberality towards all that are not of our faith, than what they exercise towards one another. These principles approximate nearer to the mind of God, because it is like God, or Godlike.[34]

Joseph Smith, the Prophet, also defended the Constitution and wrote of the greatness of the Constitution to all of those who are underprivileged.

. . . Hence we say, that the Constitution of the United States is a glorious standard; it is founded in the wisdom of God. It is a heavenly banner, it is to all those who are privileged with the sweets of its liberty, like the cooling shades and refreshing waters of a great rock in a thirsty and weary land. It is like a great tree under whose branches men from every clime can be shielded from the burning rays of the sun.

---

[32]*Ibid.*, pp. 296-97.
[33]D&C 121:33.
[34]HC 3:304.

We, brethren, are deprived of the protection of its glorious principles, by the cruelty of the cruel. . . .

But notwithstanding we see what we see, and feel what we feel, and know what we know, yet that fruit is no less precious and delicious to our taste. . . .

. . . Neither will we deny our religion because of the hand of oppression; but we will hold on until death.[35]

The Prophet's Great Influence

Will you picture with me for a moment one Levi Hancock, a representative Mormon refugee. He and his family left Missouri to make their way to Illinois. They had inadequate food, clothing, and shelter. Rags were wrapped around their feet as a protection against the cold.[36]

With Missouri behind them, they crossed the Mississippi River and found shelter. I have often wondered what the impact would have been if at that moment Levi Hancock could have read Joseph Smith's great epistle. I think a tired, weary, discouraged Levi Hancock would have drawn up a little taller, would have set his face to the future, and would have quietly said, "Yes, Brother Joseph, nothing can stop us from building God's Kingdom." This is the very thing that happened to individual Saints—as a body they were inspired by the amazing faith and strength of the Prophet. The Joseph who emerged from the Liberty Jail after almost five months of imprisonment was an even greater Joseph than the one who had entered. Why? Because under trying circumstances the greatness of his mind, the greatness of his soul, became apparent; and he communed with God.

What would have been the consequences if Joseph had manifest less strength, less hope, and less courage in a time of crisis? In my estimation, if in a few moments one wants to really come to know Joseph Smith, the best place to find out is from that remarkable general epistle written from the Liberty Jail in March of 1839. The Prophet concludes it with the

---

[35]*Ibid.*
[36]*Improvement Era*, Vol. 5, pp. 375-76.

powerful testimony which was then and still is a source of strength and inspiration to the Saints of God.

. . .We say that God is true; that the Constitution of the United States is true; that the Bible is true; that the Book of Mormon is true; that the Book of Covenants is true; that Christ is true; that the ministering angels sent forth from God are true, and that we know that we have a house not made with hands eternal in the heavens, whose builder and maker is God. . . .[37]

This experience in the life of Joseph—though not as impressive or dramatic as the first vision, or the visitation of Moroni, or the coming of Peter and James and John, or the vision in the Kirtland Temple—in an unusual and remarkable way, shows clearly the faith, courage, and greatness of Joseph Smith, his attitude, his behavior, and his example which had a profound influence upon the Church in 1839 and has had lasting influence upon the Church and its members from that day to this.

There were those who were predicting that the Church could not survive the destruction in Missouri. I have often wondered what the outcome would have been if Joseph Smith had been a lesser man, a lesser prophet.

---

[37]HC 3:304.

3 THE REAL JOSEPH SMITH

Joseph Smith's Unswerving Course

The Prophet Joseph Smith had an amazing capacity to live in a mundane, worldly environment and a sublime other-world environment simultaneously. Many are overcome by the world—not so with Joseph.

The Prophet moved with equal freedom and expertness in the temporal realm and in the spiritual realm.

The temporal was always with him, and it demanded attention. He worked the soil with his hands, cut trees, built houses, struggled to obtain money to provide the needs of his wife and children. Providing the necessary things to sustain physical life was always very much a part of him and needed constant, careful attention. Yet he was able to meet this fatherly responsibility almost as he conversed with heavenly beings and translated manuscripts and preached sermons and received inspiration for individuals and the kingdom of God on the earth. He was also able to encounter a generous amount of the vileness of the earth and encounter it continually—wrath, untruths, profanities, obscenities, vulgarities, threats, and violence. He was a constant target of the mean and low, those who were small of soul. He could hear the oaths and witness the sometimes hellish behavior, yet this did not overcome him. He could move freely from contact with the vile to the sublimity of the spiritual realm.

In a remarkable way he gave full attention to the things

which were great and small, to things which were rewarding and things necessary but somewhat unrewarding.

To a college student, President Marion D. Hanks said, "Plow wide fields as you go—never get too busy or too important to stop and help someone along the way." Joseph was a prime example of this amazing flexibility—from vision to chopping wood and back to the spiritual realm; from translating to a pressing problem that his wife had and back to translating again; from receiving a revelation to the offensive harangue of prison guards and back to revelation again. Lesser men would have been distracted from one or the other. They would have become discouraged or irritated.

Joseph Smith just plainly and simply refused to be distracted from his assigned task, a task which had been given to him directly by God—the task of restoring the fullness of the everlasting gospel and building the kingdom of God in the latter days.

Nehemiah was enticed to come down from the wall but would not—his eyes were on his task. Joseph Smith was enticed time and time again, but he refused to deviate. A mental image comes to mind—a resolute Joseph is advancing toward the goal and then a blinding, choking smokescreen is thrown up directly across his path. When the smokescreen passes, the same Joseph is still moving in the same direction. His course has not varied in the slightest degree, his step, still firm, his expression a bit more determined.

Others would have retreated, or ceased moving, or changed course, but not Joseph. His advance through obstacles of persecution, apostasy, poverty, physical pain, sorrow, and frustrated plans was for the most part totally undeviating. His example is one that we could well emulate when an obstacle in our path would make us lose sight of a goal. So often in life sickness, disappointment, death, sorrow, Satan's power would obscure our judgment and cause us to lose sight of our objectives and fall into obscurity by the side of the path as so many have before.

Joseph Smith was truly a great soul. It seems that almost

no heavenly principle was too large or complex to be comprehended by his mind and that no earthly thing was too small to escape his attention and concern. He seems to have captured a quality of true greatness and humility exemplified by Jesus who beheld heavenly beings, communed with his Father, and also talked with children and women of the street whom lesser men would have sent away. The Lord Jesus Christ, the greatest of all, the Savior of the world, knelt and washed the feet of his apostles.

Joseph Smith's judgment was remarkable, his concentration astonishing. How does one have so many distractions and still pursue an unswerving course toward a predetermined goal? With this amazing concentration and dedication, sickness, death of loved ones, poverty, harrassment, lawsuits, beatings, not even the devil himself could dissuade Joseph Smith from his course This ability ultimately made him stronger. He increased spiritually and became more intelligent in human relations and more human in intellectual pursuits. Joseph did not abandon any of his roles; hence, the great depth to his mind and soul. This takes a unique man. Some would give up and do only that which clammered most for attention.

A Greatness of Soul

Joseph Smith was a prophet of God. His greatness did not lie alone in prophesying, translating, speaking, or writing, but in what he was—he lived as a prophet. A man's true greatness is not in what he says he is, nor in what people say he is; his greatness lies in what he really is. What he really is may be determined by how he acts in those unguarded moments alone with his family or his friends. What an opportunity we would miss as students of the Prophet Joseph if we did not look as far as possible into the quiet moments, the imtimate moments of personal association of the Prophet with his wife, children, parents, brothers and sisters, and friends. It is of course more difficult to view Joseph as a family member than it is to view him as a public leader. But he included enough in his history so that we can discover the real Joseph Smith.

Joseph Smith's behavior was just as circumspect in his home as it was in public life. John M. Bernhisel, a man known for his integrity, wrote the following:

Having been a boarder in General Smith's family for more than nine months, and having therefore had abundant opportunities of contemplating his character and observing his conduct, I have concluded to give you a few of my "impressions" of him.

General Joseph Smith is naturally a man of strong mental powers, and is possessed of much energy and decision of character, great penetration, and a profound knowledge of human nature. He is a man of calm judgment, enlarged views, and is eminently distinguished by his love of justice. He is kind and obliging, generous and benevolent, sociable and cheerful, and is possessed of a mind of a contemplative and reflective character. He is honest, frank, fearless, and independent.

But it is in the gentle charities of domestic life, as the tender and affectionate husband and parent, the warm and sympathizing friend, that the prominent traits of his character are revealed and his heart is felt to be keenly alive to the kindest and softest emotions of which human nature is susceptible. . . . As a religious teacher, as well as a man, he is greatly beloved by his people. . . .[1] (Italics added.)

J. R. Wakefield, a physician, was also impressed with the Prophet as a father and felt that others could well emulate his behavior.

. . .Furthermore, having remained for a few weeks at General Smith's house, I think it is my duty to state that I have seen nothing in his deportment but what is correct in all his domestic relations, *being a kind husband and an affectionate father;* and all his affairs, both domestic and official, have not only been free from censure, but praiseworthy, and ought to be imitated by everyone desirous of order and peace.[2] (Italics added.)

Orson Pratt is another who had the privilege of viewing not only the Prophet's public life, but also his private life; and he wrote of that experience as follows:

I had the great privilege when I was in from my missions of boarding most of the time at his house, so that I not only knew him

---

[1]HC 6:468.
[2]*Ibid.*, p. 469.

as a public teacher, but as a private citizen, as a husband and father. *I witnessed his earnest and humble devotions both norning and evening in his family.* I heard the words of eternal life flowing from his mouth, nourishing, soothing, and comforting his family, neighbors, and friends.[3] (Italics added.)

And finally the following excellent and succinct observation of Wilford Woodruff:

I have felt to rejoice exceedingly in what I saw of brother Joseph, for in his public and private career he carried with him the Spirit of the Almighty, and *he manifested a greatness of soul which I had never seen in any other man.*[4] (Italics added.)

Joseph Smith had learned to live and live well. His teachings were sublime only because he lived as he taught, and his teachings came from a heart free of guilt. Joseph Smith could give outstanding teachings on love and charity because he truly was a person of compassion. He could teach forgiveness because he was forgiving. He practiced first and preached afterwards.

The Lord, speaking to Samuel, the Old Testament prophet, said, ". . .For the Lord seeth not as man seeth; for man looketh on the outward appearance, but the Lord looketh on the heart."[5] When God looked upon Joseph, He saw a faithful, worthy heart filled with love and desire to serve God and fellowmen. It is important to be a great prophet, but one cannot be a great prophet without being a great man. "For of the abundance of the heart his mouth speaketh."[6]

Emma—the Choice of My Heart

The Prophet, writing in his journal in August, 1842, reveals his deep love for his wife, Emma, as he records the events of a previous evening:

. . .with what unspeakable delight, and what transports of joy swelled my bosom when I took by the hand, on the night, *my beloved Emma—she that was my wife, even the wife of my youth, and the choice of my heart.* Many were the reverberations of my mind

---

[3]JD 7:176.
[4]*Ibid.,* p. 101.
[5]1 Samuel 16:7.
[6]Luke 6:45.

when I contemplated for a moment the many scenes we had been called to pass through, the fatigues and the toils, the sorrows and sufferings, and the joys and consolations, from time to time, which had strewed our paths and crowned our board. Oh what a commingling of thought filled my mind for the moment, again she is here, even in the seventh trouble—undaunted, firm, and unwavering— unchangeable, affectionate Emma.[7] (Italics added.)

Prior to the previously appointed time that Joseph Smith was to receive the Book of Mormon plates from the heavenly messenger Moroni, he met, fell in love with, and married Emma Hale.

What a blessing it was for the young prophet to have the assistance and strength of a wife before assuming the great responsibility of translating the Book of Mormon plates, and what a commentary it is on the goodness and integrity of Emma Hale that she would marry Joseph at this time of persecution in his life—persecution and hardship that he and she knew would never cease.

Joseph Smith fell in love with Emma while boarding at her father's home in Harmony, Pennsylvania. The courtship continued throughout his life. Perhaps we have stressed other more spectacular aspects of the life of Joseph Smith to the exclusion of his role as a husband and a father. Joseph Smith was a devoted, loving husband. There were those many occasions when an ever-present necessity to work to provide for his family took him away from them, and there were those many times when a call from God took him away, and sometimes the meanness of his fellow men kept him from his beloved wife. But when the decision was his to make, and if it were within the realm of possibility, Joseph Smith was with his companion to nurse tenderly day after day or to ride out quietly with her to see the budding trees or the maturing crops and to take her by the arm and attend a social function. Emma Hale was a beautiful woman and a worthy companion. Joseph Smith treated her with the love and respect that all husbands should show their wives.

---

[7]HC 5:107.

The Prophet Joseph Smith put into his journal many comments on his association with his wife. Sometimes the comments seem to be there by design and other times they just seem to be entered spontaneously because his life and the life of his wife are so completely intertwined.

Following are some randomly selected entries from the Prophet's journal.

Rode out with Emma and visited my farm; returned about 11 a.m., and spent the remainder of the day at home.[8]

In the evening rode out in my carriage with Emma.[9]

In the evening went with Emma to visit Elder Cahoon, where I met my brother Hyrum and his wife?[10]

Walked to the store with Emma. . . .[11]

Spend the forenoon chiefly in conversation with Emma on various subjects . . . both felt in good spirits and very cheerful.[12]

Rode to Willoughby, in company with my wife, to purchase some goods at William Lyon's store.[13]

Afternoon rode to the Grove with Emma; and attended the Female Relief Society Meeting.[14]

I rode out with Emma in a sleigh.[15]

After meeting I rode out with Emma—the trees begin to bud forth.[16]

In the afternoon I rode out with Emma . . . the peach trees look beautiful.[17] (Italics added.)

The foregoing journal entries are happy ones. There were other occasions when the entries concerning his wife were not happy entries but poignant ones. In the autumn of 1842, Emma Smith became seriously ill, and the Prophet's comments, though very simple and very brief, are most revealing.

Thursday, 29. This day Emma began to be sick with fever; consequently I kept in the house with her all day.[18]

8*Ibid.*, p. 307.
9*Ibid.*, p. 360.
10*Ibid.*, p. 525.
11*Ibid.*, p. 21.
12*Ibid.*, p. 92.
13*Ibid.*, 2:290.
14*Ibid.*, 5:139.
15*Ibid.*, 6:170.
16*Ibid.*, p. 274.
17*Ibid.*, p. 326.
18*Ibid.*, 5:166.

Friday 30. Emma is no better. I was with her all day.[19]

Saturday. October 1. This morning I had a very severe pain in my left side, and was not able to be about. Emma sick as usual.[20]

Sunday 2. Emma continued very sick. I was with her all day.[21]

Monday 3. Emma was a little better. I was with her all day.[22]

Tuesday 4. Emma is very sick again. I attended with her all the day, being somewhat poorly myself. [23]

Wednesday 5. My dear Emma was worse. Many fears were entertained that she would not recover. . . . I was unwell and much troubled on account of Emma's sickness.[24]

Thursday 6. Emma is better. . .she appears considerably easier. May the Lord speedily raise her to the bosom of her family, that the heart of His servant may be comforted again. Amen. My health is comfortable.[25]

Friday 7. *Emma is somewhat better. I am cheerful and well.*[26] (Italics added.)

Monday 10. Emma gaining slowly. My health and spirits are good.[27]

Tuesday, November 1, 1842. I rode with Emma to the Temple for the benefit of her health. She is rapidly gaining.[28]

Thursday 3. Rode out with Emma to the Temple.[29]

The entries are brief, but what a story of anxiety, love, and devotion is told in those entries in the Prophet's journal. Emma's health and well-being become a barometer of the Prophet's own health and feelings. A multiplicity of pressing duties are postponed and Joseph Smith remains at the side of his wife day after day.

The following month, one day after Christmas, Emma Smith gave birth to a son; but the child did not survive. How often had this kind of tragedy come into the life of the Prophet and his wife, Emma.

---

[19]*Ibid.*
[20]*Ibid.*
[21]*Ibid.*, p. 167.
[22]*Ibid.*
[23]*Ibid.*
[24]*Ibid.*, p. 168.
[25]*Ibid.*
[26]*Ibid.*, p. 169.
[27]*Ibid.*
[28]*Ibid.*, p. 182.
[29]*Ibid.*, p. 183.

Joseph and Emma had many occasions to weep together. Emma was ill much in child-bearing. Grief, the kind of grief that is only present with the serious illness or death of a child, came again and again in the lives of these two people.

The Prophet and His Children

The Prophet and his wife had six children, five natural and one adopted, who did not survive infancy. A son died in 1828, twins—a boy and girl—died in 1831, an adopted son died in 1832, and sons died in 1841 and 1842. They had five children, four natural sons and an adopted daughter, who lived to maturity. Emma gave birth to her last child at the age of forty—five months after the Prophet's death. When Joseph was taken in death, he left behind five children but was reunited with six others who had preceded him in death. The Prophet loved his children and recorded many activities with them. Following are some random quotations from him.

I rode out to the farm with my children, and did not return until after dark.[30]

After dinner I rode out in company with my wife and children . . . . We visited Bro. Roundy and family. . . . We had an interesting visit.[31]

In the morning I took my children on a pleasure ride in the carriage.[32]

Rode to the farm with my daughter Julia.[33]

Enjoyed myself at home with my family, all day, it being Christmas. . . .[34]

Spent the day at home in the enjoyment of the society of my family.[35]

I rode out with my family in the carriage.[36]

Remained at home and had great joy with my family.[37]

Spent the evening around my fireside teaching my family grammar.[38]

---

[30]*Ibid.*, 5:182.
[31]*Ibid.*, 2:297-98.
[32]*Ibid.*, 5:369.
[33]*Ibid.*, p. 515
[34]*Ibid.*, 2:345.
[35]*Ibid.*, p. 405.
[36]*Ibid.*, 5:500.
[37]*Ibid.*, 2:45.
[38]*Ibid.*, p. 307.

My family sang hymns and Elder John Taylor prayed and gave an address. . . .[39]

At four in the afternoon I went out with my little Frederick to exercise myself by sliding on the ice.[40] (Italics added.)

. . .After a conversation of two hours, I accompanied the brethren and Emma to my house, remaining there a few minutes to offer a blessing upon the heads of my sleeping children. . .on my way to my retreat.[41]

While imprisioned and deprived of the companionship of his wife and children for many months, the Prophet wrote the following to his wife:

My dear Emma, I very well know your toils and sympathize with you. If God will spare my life once more to have the privilege of taking care of you, I will ease your care and endeavor to comfort your heart. I want you to take the best care of the family you can which I believe you will do all you can. I was sorry to learn that Frederick was sick, but I trust he's well again and that you are all well.

I want you to try to gain time and write to me a long letter and tell me all you can and even if old Major is alive yet and what those little prattlers say that cling around your neck.[42]

It seems that the Prophet in treating his wife and children with love and respect and tenderness was emulating the behavior that he had seen in his own home as a child and a young man. He had been taught well.

Family Ties Became Closer

It is normal, it is natural, for a son to feel love and affection for his father and mother. It is normal, it is natural, for a brother to feel love and affection for his brothers and sisters. But Joseph's love and affection for members of his family seemed to exceed that of most.

Joseph could recall as a child his serious illness—the days were long, and he cried out in pain—the drawn, yet cheerful face of his mother looking down anxiously upon him:

---

[39] *Ibid.,* 6:80.
[40] *Ibid.,* 5:265.
[41] *Ibid.,* p. 160.
[42] "Church Section," *Deseret News,* April 27, 1968. p. 3.

the faithful, devoted Hyrum, six years his senior, sitting hour after hour with Joseph's infected, pain-wracked leg cradled in his hands bringing some relief to his younger brother; and the screams of his mother as she rushed into the room during the operation to see her suffering son lying in blood as the doctors removed a piece of bone from his leg. There was no anesthetic, and Joseph had refused to drink the whiskey which might have given some relief.[43] Joseph appreciated the kindness and sympathy of his family in the most painful experience. But perhaps Joseph appreciated even more the acceptance by his parents and brothers and sisters, readily and without hesitation, of his witness that he saw the Father and the Son, his witness that he had beheld an angel and viewed ancient Golden Plates. Neighbors laughed and friends scorned him. But within the walls of the Smith home there was trust, understanding, and comfort. As the years passed, the family ties became closer—the family unit more cohesive —as all worked together to provide food and clothing, to clear land, to build a house, and to strenghten each other as they were attacked by others because of what one of the young sons, Joseph, claimed to have seen and heard.

Joseph Smith deeply loved and respected his parents. This fact is unmistakable as one reads the following words of the Prophet:

I have remembered scenes of my childhood. I have thought of my father who is dead. He was a great and a good man. . . . He was of noble stature and possessed a high, and holy, and exalted, and virtuous mind. His soul soared above all those mean and groveling principles that are so congenial to the human heart. I now say that he never did a mean act, that might be said was ungenerous in his life, to my knowledge. *I love my father and his memory; and the memory of his noble deeds rests with ponderous weight upon my mind,* and many of his kind and parental words to me are written on the tablet of my heart.

Sacred to me are the thoughts which I cherish of the history of his life. . . . Let the memory of my father eternally live. . . .

Words and language are inadequate to express the gratitude that I owe to God for having given me so honorable a parentage.

<hr>

[43]HJS pp. 54-58.

My mother also is one of the noblest and best of all women. May God grant to prolong her days and mind, that we may live to enjoy each other's society long. . . .[44] (Italics added.)

The Prophet not only honored his parents with his words and with his pen, but also honored them by being concerned, assisting them, and caring for them. This is revealed by entries in the Prophet's journal:

My father and mother called this evening to see me. . . . I invited them to come and live with me. They consened to do so as soon as it was practicable.[45]

Went to visit my father, found him very low. . . .May God grant to restore him immediately to health for Christ the Redeemer's sake. Amen.[46]

At home. I attended on my father with great anxiety.[47]

At home. Waited on my father.[48]

At home, and visited the house of my father, found him failing very fast.[49]

Waited on my father again, who was very sick. In secret prayer in the morning, the Lord said, 'My servant, thy father shall live.' I waited on him all this day with my heart raised to God in the name of Jesus Christ, that He would restore him to health, *that I might be blessed with his company and advice, esteeming it one of the greatest earthly blessings to be blessed with the society of parents, whose mature years and experience render them capable of administering the most wholesome advice.* At evening Brother David Whitmer came in. We called on the Lord in mighty prayer in the name of Jesus Christ, and laid our hands on him, and rebuked the disease. And God heard and answered our prayers—to the great joy and satisfaction of our souls. Our aged father arose and dressed himself, shouted, and praised the Lord.[50] (Italics added.)

Visited my father, who was very much recovered from his sickness.[51]

The same tender concern which the Prophet manifested for his father in illness is also manifest for his mother.

---

[44]HC 5:126.
[45]*Ibid.*, 2:338.
[46]*Ibid.*, p. 288.
[47]*Ibid.*, p. 289.
[48]*Ibid.*
[49]*Ibid.*
[50]*Ibid.*, p. 289.
[51]*Ibid.*, p. 290.

Mother came to my house to live.[52]

At home all day. My mother was sick with inflammation of the lungs and I nursed her. . . .[53]

I nursed my mother most of the day, who continued very sick.[54]

Mostly with my mother and family.[55]

Rode out with mother and others for her health.[56]

I stayed home all day to take care of my mother, who was still sick.[57]

Blessed is my mother, for her soul is ever filled with benevolence and philanthropy; and notwithstanding her age, yet she shall receive strength, and shall be comforted in the midst of her house, and she shall have eternal life.[58]

Beloved Brother Hyrum

In the latter-day work Hyrum Smith stood next to his younger brother, the Prophet Joseph Smith. He was the Assistant President of the Church. He had had bestowed upon him all of the keys of the kingdom. In addition, he held the office of the Presiding Patriarch, an office which his father held prior to his death. Hyrum was second only to Joseph and was ever near him to be a source of strength and wisdom. The Prophet said of his devoted brother on one occasion:

And I could pray in my heart that all my brethren were like unto my beloved brother Hyrum, who possesses the mildness of a lamb, and the integrity of a Job, and in short, the meekness and humility of Christ; *and I love him with that love that is stronger than death*, for I never had occasion to rebuke him, nor him me.[59] (Italics added.)

Again he said of Hyrum:

There was Brother Hyrum who next took me by the hand—a natural brother. Thought I to myself, Brother Hyrum, what a faithful heart you have got! Oh may the Eternal Jehovah crown eternal

---

[52]*Ibid.*, 5:271.

[53]*Ibid.*, p. 290.

[54]*Ibid.*

[55]*Ibid.*

[56]*Ibid.*, 6:65.

[57]*Ibid.*, 5:298.

[58]*Ibid.*, 1:466.

[59]*Ibid.*, 2:338.

blessings upon your heart, as a reward for the care you have had for my soul! O how many are sorrows we have shared together; and again we find ourselves shackled with the unrelenting hand of oppression. *Hyrum, thy name shall be written in the book of the law of the Lord, for those who come after thee to look upon, that they may pattern after thy works.*[60] (Italics added.)

The foregoing tributes by Joseph are not only a commentary of the greatness of Hyrum, his brother, but are also commentaries on the Prophet's capacity to love and appreciate. This love and appreciation also extended to other brothers, and he pays tribute to two of them who preceeded him in death:

Expressions of Love and Gratitude

Alvin, my oldest brother—*I remember well the pangs of sorrow that swelled my youthful bosom and almost burst my tender heart when he died. He was the oldest and the noblest of my father's family.* He was one of the noblest of the sons of men. . . .In him there was no guile. He lived without spot from the time he was a child. . . and when he died the angel of the Lord visited him in his last moments.[61]

My brother Don Carlos Smith. . .was a noble boy; I never knew any fault in him. . . .he was lovely, a good natured, a kind-hearted and a virtuous and a faithful, upright child; *and where his soul goes, let mine go also.*[62] (Italics added.)

The Prophet, in a letter to his brother William, mentions all of the members of his family and invokes God's blessings that they may enjoy each other forever:

. . .And now may God have mercy upon my father's house. . . bring us both to Thee, O God, and to Thy power and protection, to enjoy the society of father, mother, Alvin, Hyrum, Sophronia, Samuel, Catherine, Carlos, Lucy, and all the sanctified in peace, forever.[63]

The Family Is Eternal

It seems appropriate for one who appreciates loved ones

[60]*Ibid.*, 5:107-108.
[61]*Ibid.*, p. 126.
[62]*Ibid.*, p. 127.
[63]*Ibid.*, 2:343.

so much that such a one would be chosen by God to receive not only the revelations from God, but the power, the sealing power, to make what had been a transitory thing an everlasting thing, a temporary thing a permanent thing. No more would the family unit have to cease to be because of the intervention of death, often the happenstance intervention of death. Now on the earth was the power, the divine sealing power, to assure that family life would be continued forever, eternally. What extreme joy must have been the Prophet Joseph's as he learned and received the power and authority. How it must have pleased him to tell his kindly mother, his faithful father, and his brothers and sisters. How it must have eased the pain of separation from the remarkable Alvin to know that in the future all of the Joseph Smith, Sr., family could again be reunited. And how the knowledge, restored by God through his Prophet Joseph, has brought comfort and even joy to numerous faithful who also have known the pain and heartbreak of separation from loved ones.

Parley P. Pratt wrote of his feeling as he was taught of the eternal nature of the family relationship by the Prophet:

In Philadelphia I had the happiness of once more meeting with President Smith, and of spending several days with him, and others, and with the saints in that city and vicinity. During these interviews he taught me many great and glorious principles concerning God and the heavenly order of eternity. It was at this time that I received from him the first idea of eternal family organization. . . . Till then I had learned to esteem kindred affections and sympathies as appertaining solely to this transitory state. . . . *It was Joseph Smith who taught me how to prize the endearing relationships of father and mother, husband and wife; of brother and sister, son and daughter.* It was from him that I learned that the wife of my bosom might be secured to me for time and all eternity. We might cultivate these affections, and grow and increase in the same to all eternity. . . .It was from him that I learned the true dignity and destiny of a son of God. . . .It was from him that I learned that the highest dignity of womanhood was to stand as a queen and princess to her husband. . . .Yet, at that time, Joseph Smith, had barely touched a single key; had merely lifted a corner of the veil and given me a single glance into eternity.[64] (Italics added.)

---

[64]*Pratt*, pp. 297-98.

The Lord Jesus Christ has always placed primary emphasis upon the home, and his servant Joseph Smith demonstrated this in his personal behavior. The Church which Joseph organized has always stressed, and continues to stress today, the importance of the family; and today we are particularly blessed because the Church has developed excellent programs and materials to assist us in this vital primary responsibility.

In the Church and in society there are so many good things to accomplish. Some of these good things can be accomplished with less demands, or at least different demands, on the individual than other things. While in Liberty Jail, Joseph Smith wrote:

No power or influence can or ought to be maintained by virtue of the priesthood, only by persuasion, by long-suffering, by gentleness and meekness, and by love unfeigned.[65]

In no situation is it more difficult to emulate these excellent qualities than in the confines of one's own home, with one's own wife and children.

Because the role of a father or mother, son or daughter, is exacting and sometimes difficult, we must be careful lest we mistakenly fill our lives with other good things which consume our time and not only ease our conscience but make us feel noble because we are so very busy. Joseph did not ignore, but joyfully accepted, his responsibility as a family member and family head.

---

[65]D&C 121:41.

4 "HE ASKED IF I FOR HIM WOULD DIE"

A City Beautiful

As the weeks continued to pass after the majority of the Latter-day Saints had fled from Missouri, the presence of Joseph Smith and his associates in Missouri prisons became an increasing source of embarrassment. The Mormon leaders were innocent of any crime, and the public officials finally determined that the best way out of this dilemma would be to permit the prisoners to escape. As Joseph and his companions were being conveyed from one jail to another, the guards indicated that in the evening would be an excellent time for the prisoners to escape because they had some "jugs" and were going to do some drinking. The prisoners protested the necessity of escaping on foot. The guards were most obliging and offered to sell horses to them. The prisoners had only enough personal belongings to purchase one horse and they insisted they needed at least two. The guards were most cooperative and said, in essence, "We know we can trust you. Give us your note and you can have another horse."[1]

Joseph, free again, determined to gather the scattered Saints to a plot of ground situated on a horseshoe bend of the Mississippi River. It was a beautiful sight, being surrounded on three sides by the same river. The city was visible for miles to those who traveled up and down the great river. Under the direction of the Prophet Joseph, the swampy

---

[1]HC 3:453.

area, renamed Nauvoo, was soon to rapidly be transformed into a lovely city. As the work of draining the swampy area where the City Beautiful would be built progressed, many, almost all, became ill with fever. The Prophet was nursed day after day. Finally, as he learned of the number of those ill, he called upon God to make him well and to permit him to be God's instrument in restoring others to health. The Prophet was made well; he arose from his bed, and went into his own dooryard where numbers of his followers were gathered. He laid his hands upon them, one after another, and through God's power they arose. He called members of the Twelve to follow him and assist him. They visited the ill in Nauvoo. As they came to Elijah Fordham, the Prophet took hold of his hand and looked at the unconscious man for a few moments and then commanded, "Brother Fordham, in the name of Jesus Christ arise and walk." He immediately arose from his bed, got dressed, called for some food, and went with the Prophet to bless and heal others.[2]

The Quorum of the Twelve was dispatched to England to teach the gospel more fully in that land, and corner stones were laid for a new and impressive temple overlooking the surrounding countryside.

The people of Illinois had kindly welcomed the persecuted Saints with open arms, and this kindness continued. It looked as though this time a dream could at least be partially fulfilled, and the Saints could gather and build a beautiful city, build a temple to their God, and live and worship without fear.

Once again this was not to be. For numerous reasons, opposition increased, and soon there were those who were calling for the overthrow of Joseph and the removal of the Mormons. And there were some who would prefer to see Joseph Smith dead. Finally, on Friday, June 7, 1844, the first and only issue of a slanderous paper was issued in Nauvoo. It was titled "The Nauvoo Expositor." The authors were

---

[2]Whitney, Orson F., *Life of Heber C. Kimball* (Salt Lake City: Stevens and Wallis, 1888), pp. 273-74. See also *Pratt*, p. 293.

apostate Mormons who were collaborating with hateful non-Mormons. Joseph Smith was mayor of the city, and immediately the city council was called into session. They met that evening, again all day Saturday, and they were in session again early Monday morning. They finally concluded, after the study of the law books, that they had a right to declare the paper a public nuisance and also had the right to abate the nuisance. They sent the city marshall to stop publication. The publishers of the Expositor immediately raised a resounding cry of obstruction of freedom of speech and freedom of the press, and a cry went up from all quarters condemning Joseph Smith and calling for his speedy trial in Carthage. Joseph Smith knew that if he went to Carthage he would never return alive. Citizens of the surrounding communities clamored for Joseph and the other members of the city council to be tried at the county seat.[3]

A Place In The West

Joseph Smith was young, strong, and vigorous. He was filled with energy and hope. He had always dreamed big dreams, very big dreams, and worked tirelessly to bring those dreams to reality. His heart and mind were still filled with dreams—dreams for his children: Julia, thirteen years old now; Joseph III, his first surviving son, eleven years old; Frederick, age eight; and Alexander, just six years old. Also, he had dreams for a child yet unborn. He had said to Emma, in essence, "If our baby is a boy, let's name him David Hyrum." Dreams, worthy dreams for his children. The older ones, as young as they were, had already experienced the terror of a mob. Their mother had walked with them across Missouri to Quincy, Illinois, in 1838 while their father was imprisoned. Joseph wanted to raise them, play with them, teach them, and have for them a place to live where there would be no hunger, no terror, but peace and safety. No, there was much to live for—so many wonderful, so many exciting things. Joseph Smith had no desire to die. He loved

[3]CHC 2:235, 236.

life. He relished it and its experiences. But it was evident that a circle of apostasy, bitterness, and hatred which threatened his very being was drawing ever tighter. At this time the Prophet said: "I told Stephen Markham that if I and Hyrum were ever taken again we should be massacred, or I was not a prophet of God."[4]

Joseph, in the presence of several of his brethren, read a letter for Governor Thomas Ford, the governor of Illinois. As the Prophet put the letter down he said, "There is no mercy—no mercy here."

Hyrum said, "No; just as sure as we fall into their hands we are dead men."

Joseph replied, "Yes; what shall we do, Brother Hyrum?"

He replied, "I don't know."

All at once Joseph's countenance brightened and he said, "The way is open. It is clear to my mind what to do. All they want is Hyrum and myself; then tell everybody to go about their business."[5]

Joseph determined at that point that he and Hyrum would go to the west and prepare a place for the Saints. What an exciting thought this was, not to be at the end of life, but the beginning of a joyful and almost limitless new experience. Joseph Smith had known for some time that the Church would move to the west. He had learned of this in a vision on August 6, 1843. Anson Call was present and wrote the following:

I had before seen him in vision, and now saw while he was talking, his countenance change to white. . .a living, brilliant white. He seemed absorbed in gazing upon the valleys of those mountains. This was followed by a vivid description of the scenery of these mountains as I have since become acquainted with it. . . .There was a force and power to his exclamation, of which the following is but a faint echo; "Oh the beauty of those snow capped mountains! The cool, refreshing strems that are running down the mountain gorges. . . ."[6]

Now that which had been seen by him—which was so

---

[4]HC 6:546.
[5]*Ibid.*, p. 545.
[6]*Ibid.*, 5:85-86.

thrilling, so filled with promise—would be realized. He and Hyrum would go west to find the place of refuge and safety for the Saints where they would be free from hurt. The Prophet's mind was working rapidly now. There would be much to do. He would have to have supplies and equipment, make arrangements for his wife and children. It would take money, and all of this would have to be accomplished immediately. The Prophet borrowed $1,000 and made arrangements with loyal friends to take his wife and children to a place of safety and await word from him. He crossed the river that very night to gather the supplies together and prepare to leave. The next morning messengers came from Nauvoo. The Prophet was ill prepared for the word that they brought. He had never shirked his responsibility as a servant of the Lord from the time he had had a vision that spring day twenty-four years before. He had been arrested, beaten, and harassed, and he had almost never faltered. Hadn't he been an example to his followers—hadn't he been faithful to the Lord Jesus Christ? Shouldn't his followers know that? He was stunned as the messengers asked him to return. As they did so, they gave him a letter from Emma which also entreated him to come back and face the charges.

A Prophet's Last Goodbye

The Prophet had been packing as the messengers entered the room. He stood stunned, and he was told that he was like a shepherd deserting his flock in the face of danger.[7] Joseph Smith was being accused of cowardice. How does one who has hardly known fear react to a charge of cowardice? He turned to Porter Rockwell and said, "Porter, what shall we do?" Perhaps the Prophet, now broken-hearted, was trying to gain perspective and balance in a situation which had almost totally devastated him. Porter said, "I do not know. You are older than I. You will have to decide." He then turned to Hyrum, the one who had always been able to help him, and said, "Hyrum, what shall I do?" Hyrum said, "Let's go back.

[7]*Ibid.,* 6:549-50.

I think all will be well with us." Joseph's reply was significant: "If my life is of no value to my friends, my life is of no value to me." And preparations were made for the return to Nauvoo.

It was a melancholy Joseph Smith who returned to Nauvoo to make the arrangements to go to Carthage. He knew, he was the only one who knew that this would be the last time he would look on his beloved city, Nauvoo. He rode to his farm and said, "This is the loveliest place and the best people under the heavens." He looked upon the temple which was now up to the square, and he went to say goodbye to his wife and children. He was solemn and thoughtful. He embraced them. Perhaps they wondered why it was so hard for their father to leave them and why he returned again and embraced them each once more and again told them goodbye. He knew why the parting was so difficult for him. They did not know. How does one say goodbye to his wife and children for the last time—the very last time? Finally he was astride his horse and rode with his brother and others away from his house and toward Carthage. A faint wave of his arm, and he was lost from view. As he rode he soberly said, "I am going like a lamb to the slaughter, but I am calm as a summer's morning. I have a conscience void of offense toward God and toward all men. If they take my life I shall die an innocent man, and it shall be said of me, 'He was murdered in cold blood!' "[8]

Carthage

Joseph and Hyrum rode together toward Carthage. It was a fateful ride. Joseph had tried in vain to persuade his beloved brother to remain behind, but he would not. S. Dilworth Young portrays in poetry the bond between the brothers.

> . . .Hyrum rides with me.
> His loyalty transcends,
> Exalts, the common blood
> We share. . . .

He is not sure, not yet,
Of what we face, as I am sure,
And that is best.
Why don't I send him back?
Command in God's own name?

He might obey me and find rest
Safe rest,
Among the saints.
But no, we're bound
Together now with bands
Like steel:
The banks of love,
The banks of blood,
The bands of waking and of
Sleeping,
The bands of sorrow and of
Weeping,
The bands of happiness and joy.
He stays with me, though he
Is free
To go,
And he will be with me
Eternally.[9]

It was late, very late, when Joseph, Hyrum, and other members of the city council arrived at Carthage, the county seat of Hancock County. It had taken Joseph a long time to say his goodbyes.

The following morning, Governor Ford arranged to have the Prophet pass before the troops so that they could all see him. Later in the morning, a delegation of officers came to visit the Prophet and his fellow prisoners. During the interview, the Prophet in essence said, "Tell me, gentlemen, do I look like the desperate character that I am proported to be?" The reply: "No sir, you do not, but we cannot see what is in your heart"; to which Joseph gravely replied, "That is true, gentlemen, but I can see what is in your hearts, and will tell you what I see. I can see blood, and nothing but my blood with satisfy you."[10]

---

[9]Young, S. Dilworth, *The Long Road from Vermont to Carthage* (Salt Lake City: Bookcraft, 1967), pp. 177-78.
[10]HC 6:566.

The hearing was held, and the prisoners were bound over for trial and released on bond. Joseph and Hyrum, however, were immediately charged with another crime—the charge was treason and they were not permitted to leave for Nauvoo, but were returned to the jail. The charge of treason stemmed from the fact that Joseph, as Mayor of Nauvoo, had declared martial law and had called out Nauvoo Legion troops to protect the city. This had only been done after extensive correspondence with Governor Ford, and the governor was the person who had suggested that if the situation deteriorated, martial law might have to be declared. Now Joseph and Hyrum were detained for following that suggestion. Governor Ford gave Joseph Smith his solemn pledge that if he left Carthage, Joseph Smith would go with him. The governor left for Nauvoo without Joseph Smith, even though he had been told, and was retold as he left the city, the great danger the Prophet would be in if he did not accompany him. Governor Ford, however, did not heed the warning.

While imprisoned, Joseph bore a powerful testimony to those who guarded him. He told them of the Book of Mormon, the restoration of the gospel, and the visitation of angels.[11] As Joseph retired to bed, he again stated that he was to die and said, "I would like to see my family again" and "I would to God that I could preach to the Saints in Nauvoo once more."[12]

Samuel Smith sought desperately to get to Carthage to assist his imprisoned brothers, but he was turned back by those who guarded the road. He finally returned to his house, took almost all he had and traded it for an extremely fast horse, and approached the guards again at a leisurely pace. Suddenly he whipped his horse, dashed past the astonished guards, and soon outdistanced his pursuers; but he did not arrive in time to assist or comfort his brothers.[13]

---

[11]*Ibid.*, p. 600.
[12]*Ibid.*, pp. 600-601.
[13]Journal History, July 25, 1844.

That Fateful Day

It was late in the afternoon of a sultry summer day, June 27, 1844. Joseph had sent a final message to his wife:

Dear Emma, I am very much resigned to my lot, knowing I am justified, and have done the best that can be done. Give my love to the children and all my friends.[14]

There were only four who now remained: Joseph the Prophet; his ever devoted brother Hyrum, assistant president of the Church and presiding patriarch; John Taylor, the stalwart convert from Canada, an apostle; and Willard Richards, also a member of the Quorum of the Twelve, a physician and the Prophet's secretary.

John Taylor was asked to sing. He sang "A Poor Wayfaring Man of Grief." Apparently the message of the song—the words about the Lord and Savior Jesus Christ—were comforting and strengthening to Joseph Smith, because a few minutes later Brother Taylor was requested to sing the song again. The third from the last verse is particularly significant:

My friendship's utmost zeal to try
He asked if I for him would die
The blood ran chill, but the free spirit cried "I Will."[15]

Joseph did not want to die. There was so much to live for. Just as the Savior's response was "not my will, but thy will be done," so Joseph Smith's response to the Lord and Savior in life and in the face of death was, "not my will, but thy will be done."

A noise was heard outside. Over one hundred men with blacked faces stormed the jail. Some remained below and shot through the windows; others rushed up the stairs. The prisoners tried to hold the wooden door against the onslaught. Hyrum was shot in the face, and as he fell, he uttered, "I am a dead man." His brother, Joseph, sprang to his side and kneeling said, "Oh my poor dear brother Hyrum." John Taylor was shot repeatedly and fell. Joseph ran toward the win-

---

[14]HC 6:605.
[15]*Ibid.*, pp. 614-15.

dow, was shot, and fell from the window. His last words were, "My Lord, my God."[16]

The Latter-day Joseph was dead. A cry went up from the mob that the Mormons were coming. The information was incorrect, but they and all the residents of Carthage fled in terror, fearing that the Mormons would come to avenge the death of their leader. But once again, as so many times before, the feelings and attitudes of the followers of Joseph were misunderstood. A message, brief and pointed, was sent by the surviving, unhurt companion of Joseph, Dr. Willard Richards:

Carthage Jail, 8:05 o-clock, p.m., June 27th, 1844.

Joseph and Hyrum are dead. Taylor wounded. . . I am well. Our guard was forced as we believe by a band of Missourians from 100 to 200. The job was done in an instant, and the party fled towards Nauvoo instantly. This is as I believe it. The citizens here are afraid of the Mormons attacking them. I promise them no!

W. Richards, John Taylor[17]

The Bodies Returned to Nauvoo

When the Mormons came it was to mournfully claim the bodies of their two fallen leaders, not to seek revenge and bring destruction to Carthage and its people.

The morning after the tragedy, Willard Richards and Samuel Smith came from Nauvoo with the bodies of the martyrs. The bodies were covered with brush to shelter them from the sun. A great multitude of people met them on Mulholland Street, about a mile from the temple. It was now 3:00 p.m. The bodies were washed and prepared for burial. Joseph had been shot in the right side of his chest, also under the heart, and in his abdomen, and had also been shot from behind through the right hip. One ball had come out through the right shoulder blade. Cotton soaked in camphor was placed in each wound, and the bodies were dressed in white.[18]

---

[16]*Ibid.*, pp. 618-19.
[17]*Ibid.*, pp. 621-22.
[18]*Ibid.*, pp. 626-29.

After this was done, the wives and children of the Prophet and patriarch were permitted to see the bodies. When Emma saw the body of Joseph, she screamed and fell back; she was caught and supported. She kissed the Prophet, called his name, and begged him to speak to her once more. Mary, Hyrum's wife, was calm and composed.[19]

Thousands gathered the next day to view the bodies of the fallen latter-day prophet and his faithful brother. What a poignant scene that must have been on the memorable day. With little effort I can picture what *could* have taken place. Imagination combined with facts can produce insights.

What Manner of Man Was This Joseph Smith?

It was a warm day—the date, June 29, 1944. A boat is approaching a horseshoe bend in the Mississippi River. Situated prominently on that bend is a city. A traveler seeks to identify the city from his map, but the map which was printed a few years previously shows no such city. Upon inquiry the interested traveler is told that the city is Nauvoo and that the boat would make a brief stop there.

As the boat docks, the traveler becomes curious as to why long lines of people are waiting to enter a large home on the river front. He, being in no hurry to reach his destination, informs the captain that he is going to remain in this Nauvoo for a few hours, or perhaps overnight.

As the visitor approaches the end of the line, it becomes apparent that these are grief-stricken people. All of the ladies and many of the men are weeping. He approaches one of the mourners and inquires, "Excuse me, but what are these lines for; what are you waiting to see?"

The mourner looks at him in amazement, "You mean you don't know?"

"I'm a stranger here. I just arrived on the boat," he answers, pointing in the direction of the pier.

"Oh, I see," replies the mourner. "These people and myself are waiting to view the bodies of Lieutenant General

[19]*Ibid.*

Joseph Smith and his brother Hyrum Smith who were killed two days ago."

"*Lieutenant General* Smith?" the visitor says questioningly.

"Yes, he was the lieutenant general of a legion of five thousand men, most of them uniformed and equipped."

"How many others were killed with them?" asks the stranger.

"None," replies the mourner. "This is perhaps one of the reasons why Joseph died. He believed that it was his life that was wanted and that if he died, the lust for blood would be satisfied and others would not be killed. He wanted his brother Hyrum to live, but Hyrum insisted that he be by the side of his brother. 'In life they were not divided, and in death they were not separated.' "

The traveler asks, "How did the trouble that lead to their deaths begin?"

"The most immediate cause was the destruction of the printing press of the *Nauvoo Expositor*," replies the mourner. "The *Expositor* was owned by the enemies of Joseph Smith, and they published a libelous paper. An order to close the paper was issued by the city council and the mayor, Joseph Smith."

"Joseph Smith was the *mayor* of this city?"

"Yes, he was," comes the reply.

"This is a very new city, isn't it?" says the stranger. "Why, it isn't even on my map."

"Yes, Yes, it is new. Why, just six years ago this was nothing but a swamp."

The traveler says, "It is a beautiful city. I noticed as I came up the river that most of the farms and corrals were outside of town."

"Yes, this is the way Joseph planned the city."

"Joseph *planned this city*?" repeats the stranger.

"Yes, so that the people, who are mostly farmers, could have the advantages of city life by all living together—so that we might associate together and learn from each other."

The traveler comments on the wide, straight streets and the well-built houses. He also tells the mourner that he has seen a large white building apparently under construction. The building is on the most prominent rise of land in the city. The mourner informs the visitor that the building is the temple and that Joseph Smith had designed it to be the dominant landmark in the city.

"Joseph Smith *designed the temple!*" the stranger exclaims.

"Yes, Joseph designed it," comes the reply.

The traveler then remembers, "You were telling me what led to the death of this Joseph Smith."

"Oh, yes, the *Expositor* incident. But the trouble began a long time ago, long before that incident, even before Joseph translated the ancient record."

"He was a *translator* of ancient languages?" repeats the visitor. "How many languages did he know?"

"I am not certain," replies the mourner, "but he knew Hebrew, German, and Egyptian."

"What happened to this translation of the ancient record?" questions the traveler.

"It has been published and it is called the Book of Mormon."

The traveler continues to question, "Has he published any other books?"

"Oh, yes, as president of the Church————"

"*President* of the Church————?"

"Yes, president of The Church of Jesus Christ of Latter-day Saints. Almost everyone here in Nauvoo is a member of the Church.

"As I was saying," continues the mourner, "as president of the Church he published the Doctrine and Covenants."

"What kind of book is that?" asks the amazed visitor.

"It is a book of revelations which were given to the Prophet Joseph Smith by the Lord."

"The *Prophet* Joseph Smith!"

"Yes, he was a prophet. God the Father and Jesus Christ appeared to him and conversed with him. In fact, it was after Joseph, full of joy and boyish enthusiasm, told his neighbors that he had seen a vision that the persecution first began. Not only was Joseph persecuted, but also all of his followers. Why, many of the people you see about you here were driven from homes in Missouri. None of us were paid for our losses. Joseph tried in vain to obtain redress, but we were refused. That is the principle reason that Joseph became a candidate for the presidency of the United States."

"A *candidate for the presidency* of the United States!" the bewildered traveler replies.

The mourner continues: "It was four days ago that Joseph bid a reluctant farewell to his family, looked longingly at the temple and then at his farm, and said, 'This is the loveliest place and best people under the heavens,' as he rode toward the county seat at Carthage to turn himself over to his enemies. He said to those who accompanied him, 'I am going like a lamb to the slaughter, but I am as calm as a summer's morning.' He was promised protection and a fair trial, but two days ago, on June 27th, a band of over one hundred men with blackened faces stormed the Carthage jail. A few moments later they retreated, and Lieutenant General Joseph Smith and his faithful brother Hyrum lay dead."

The traveler and the mourner have now come to the door. They cease talking. The visitor strains to see the bodies. He sees two coffins, and in each, directly over the face of the occupant, is a piece of glass. The visitor looks questioningly at the mourner, who with a gesture indicates that the nearest casket contains the body of Joseph Smith.

As the stranger views the body, his face registers surprise and disbelief. He speaks almost silently, "*This* is Joseph Smith!" He sees a young man, a handsome man with a prominent nose and a slightly receding forehead. He is stunned; he had expected to see an old man with white hair and a long, flowing beard, and a face drawn and wrinkled with age. He quietly whispers to the mourner, "How old was he?"

In a subdued tone comes the reply, "He was thirty-eight years of age."

As the traveler looks almost in disbelief, he thinks, "Lieutenant general, linguist, translator, author, mayor, prophet, president, city planner, architect, presidential candidate—WHAT MANNER OF MAN WAS THIS JOSEPH SMITH?"

The silence is interrupted as a man in the corner of the room asks for the attention of the group and says, "My dear brothers and sisters, it is five o'clock. We would like to clear this room so that the loved ones of those deceased can view the bodies alone for the last time."

As the traveler and the mourner make their way out through the open door, the traveler stops to shake the mourner's hand and to thank him. When he reaches the gate he turns and begins walking in the direction of the temple.

As he walks, the same question escapes his lips: "WHAT MANNER OF MAN WAS THIS JOSEPH SMITH?"

He continues up the street and is lost from view.

Perhaps there was no stranger, but again, it *could* have happened on that warm June day in 1844.

The Unknown Grave

After the loved ones viewed the bodies for the last time, trusted friends removed the bodies from the caskets, weighted the caskets, and took them solemnly to the public cemetery for burial. The bodies were then buried secretly in the basement of the uncompleted Nauvoo House. This precaution had been made necessary by the rumor that $1,000 had been offered for the head of Joseph Smith, and the digging up and desecrating of dead bodies by their enemies was not unknown to the Saints. It had been done many times by their enemies. As time passed, the bodies were relocated. The years seemed to obscure the location of the graves, and David Hyrum, who had been born five months after the death of his father, as a young man wrote a poem honoring his father. It is entitled "The Unknown Grave."

THE UNKNOWN GRAVE
There's an unknown grave in a green, lowly spot,
The form that it covers will ne'er be forgot,
Where haven trees spread and the wild locusts wave
Their fragrant white blooms o'er the unknown grave,—
O'er the unknown grave.

And nearby its side does the wild rabbit tread,
While over its bosom the wild thistles spread,
As if, in their kindness, to guard and to save
From man's footstep, intruding, the unknown grave,—
    Guarding the unknown grave.

The heavens may weep and the thunders moan low,
Or the bright sun shine, and the soft breezes blow;
Unheeding the heart, once responsive and brave,
Of the one who sleeps there in the unknown grave,—
    Low in an unknown grave.

The prophet whose life was destroyed by his foes
Sleeps now where no hand may disturb his repose
'Til the trumpets of God drown the notes of the wave
 And we see him arise from his unknown grave,—
    God bless that unknown grave.

The love all-embracing that never can end,
In death, as in life, knew him well as a friend;
The power of Jesus, the mighty to save,
 Will despoil of its treasure the unknown grave,—
    No more an unknown grave.

—David Hyrum Smith[20]

I Wish It Could Have Been the First Prophet

Joseph did not shirk life, nor did he try to avoid its experiences. He was "a front line" leader, a "forefront-of-the-battle" prophet.

He marched, built, sawed, hewed, plowed, planted with everyone else. His muscular body was a result of physical exertion. His mind was "an IDEAL" of unrelenting seeking. His soul yearned for truth, and his personality reached out tenderly to encourage, cheer, and revitalize his fellow Saints. This permitted Joseph Smith to be measured by others, to be evaluated. He was not at a distance, but always close as a handshake.

Those who demonstrated by their lives that they had the Spirit of the Lord Jesus Christ demonstrated it by faithfulness in the Church during the life of Joseph Smith and in the years

[20]McGavin, E. Cecil, *The Family of Joseph Smith* (Salt Lake City: Bookcraft, 1963), pp. 165-66.

after. They liked what they saw; they sought to be like him.

For those who judged him by the standards of the world, Joseph Smith often came off "wanting." These left him, and some fought against him.

How could he build the kingdom of God in the last days unless he had intimate associations with his followers? Jesus had demonstrated in fishing boats and on hillsides and in cities that one, by closeness of proximity, makes enemies; but more important, one makes friends and converts.

The risk was great. Jesus was betrayed by one of his own, Judas. Joseph as well was betrayed from within by one of his own counselors.

But success must be counted in friends.

Peter, James, John, and others emerged to greatness. Peter, when brought before the Sanhedran was threatened and abused but emulated his Lord.

Brigham Young's decisive take-charge attitude in Nauvoo and his striking success emulated the vastness of dreams and hopes that Joseph had displayed. His courage in trials rivaled Joseph Smith.

Joseph Smith is the epitome of the whole, well-rounded man. Only one person would determine what he was and would be, and that was the Lord Jesus Christ. Social convention was not that which determined his behavior.

He had a zest for life. He could absorb all it had to offer and still hunger for additional experience. He faced it head on, and took its full impact and relished more, and prior to his death wanted to swing his large frame into a saddle and explore the West to find that place in the Rockies that he had seen in vision—the place of refuge for his oft-persecuted followers. Often in my mind's eye I have envisioned Brigham Young looking from Wilford Woodruff's carriage in that most dramatic moment and saying, "This is the right place, drive on." What a thrilling moment in history as the Saints had found their haven in the mountains.

Sometimes in quiet, reflectful moments, I wish it could have been the first prophet of the last dispensation, the tall young prophet not yet forty years old. I can see vividly in my mind how it might have been. He would have been dusty and tired from a long ride. He would be erect in the saddle, drinking deeply of every new object in his surroundings. And then, as he ascended the top of another mountain, another of too many to remember, he would look over the valley and know. He would swing down from his tired horse, remove his travel worn hat, and kneel reverently, thankfully before God. And how his eyes would flash as he spoke in excited terms about building a place where "the Saints could grow as large as they had a mind to." But it was not to be. How he could have liked it to be! But he had prepared well those who followed him. The same determination, the same genius, the same inspiration from the same God would be theirs.

The melancholy Joseph had to set his eyes back across the Mississippi, back toward hatred and disloyalty and death. For a fleeting moment—an unrealistic moment, and all too brief a moment—his eyes had been looking west to freedom, to adventure and to a continuation of building the kingdom of God on earth.

The resolute prophet returned—others guessed what might happen and hoped it would not.

Joseph knew what would happen and wished it would not. Again, as so often before, Joseph reached deeply into a reservoir of courage. Never before had he needed to reach so deeply, and never again would he.

In a matter of weeks, Samuel Smith joined his brothers in death. He never recovered from the exhaustion and exposure of that fateful June day.

Hyrum Smith's loyalty to his brother Joseph had caused his death. This may also be said of Samuel. Though his death was less dramatic, it came as a result of loyalty to his brother Joseph Smith. Samuel was the first missionary of the Church; and while on that first mission in the year 1830, he had borne witness that his brother Joseph Smith was a prophet of God. Now, fourteen years later, in 1844, he bore witness with his life, as had his brother Hyrum.

When Joseph bade farewell to the people in Nauvoo and started toward Carthage he was young, strong, vigorous; and it had not entered the minds of his followers that he might die. He had been in danger before, many times. Since he was fourteen he had lived with danger, but hadn't he always returned to them? This time he did not return. The people were stunned as they viewed his bullet-riddled body. Many were not only stunned, but confused. Joseph had been their leader; and now he and Hyrum, the assistant president of the Church, were dead. Some thought that Joseph would be immediately resurrected and come back to them to continue as their leader.[21] Some felt that the Church could not survive without Joseph.

Here Is Brigham

Sidney Rigdon, the member of the first presidency whom Joseph had unsuccessfully tried to remove from his position, returned from Pittsburgh. He asked that he be appointed guardian of the Church. An open-air meeting was called, and Sidney Rigdon, with William Marks at his side, ascended to the stand. The wind blowing toward them was so strong that they mounted a wagon behind the congregation, and the people turned and faced them. Sidney, who had been the great orator of the Church, was ineffective that day. Brigham Young and most of the twelve had been in the mission field when Joseph and Hyrum were killed; they returned to Nauvoo and took their place on the stand. As Sidney was speaking, the wind ceased blowing. When he had concluded, Brigham Young began to speak; and the people turned to listen.[22] Brigham Young literally devastated Sidney's claim to leadership with one sentence. He said: "Here is Brigham—have his knees ever faltered?"[23] In 1839 Brigham Young had risked his life to return to Far West to the midst of his enemies so that a prophecy made by Joseph Smith could be fulfilled. In the autumn of that same year, he left for a mission to England

---

[21]JD 23:363-64.
[22]*Ibid.*
[23]Young, S. Dilworth, *Here is Brigham* (Salt Lake City: Bookcraft, 1964), p. 361.

where he had to be lifted into a wagon because he was so ill. Well could he say, "Have his knees ever faltered?" In contrast, Sidney's knees had faltered almost continuously since the Saints had left Missouri. What Brigham Young was, was known to the Saints. As he spoke, numerous beheld a miracle which was a witness of their faith. Before them again was the Prophet Joseph. Brigham Young looked and sounded like Joseph Smith. As surely as the mantle of authority which Elijah had fell upon Elisha, so surely had the mantle of Joseph Smith fallen upon Brigham Young.

The Lord in his mercy had again in an unmistakable manner directed his people. It was not the church of Joseph Smith. It was the Church of Jesus Christ. He had directed his Prophet Joseph to bestow the keys of authority upon the Twelve, and now he showed his followers that the Twelve, with Brigham Young as the president of that quorum, were to lead the Church. Brigham Young asked the thousands assembled if they would sustain the Twelve. The voting was unanimous. A few days later Sidney Ridgon left Nauvoo for Pittsburgh, drawing a handful of followers with him. The Twelve renamed the City of Nauvoo the City of Joseph, and they encouraged the Saints to complete the temple as a monument to the name of Joseph Smith. Joseph Smith was dead, but the Church of Jesus Christ was very much alive.

5 JOSEPH SMITH: AN EVALUATION

Joseph Smith Relished Life

I have mentally rehearsed the life of the Prophet Joseph Smith, trying to think of an incident that would even give a hint of cowardice. I know of none. On the other hand, incidents of courage are almost endless. Joseph Smith seriously accepted the responsibility of restoring the kingdom of God to the earth. It was a large task, but God was the author of it. Joseph was totally dedicated to the building of the kingdom and the achievement of its ultimate destiny of filling the entire earth.

He was completely involved in the progress of the Church. He was consumed by an idea, and what others may have perceived as devastating if not fatal blows to the kingdom, Joseph Smith saw as temporary setbacks to a cause which could not be stopped. Joseph Smith refused to be placed on the defensive, although the odds against success often seemed insurmountable. He retained the initiative.

In spite of brutal treatment and heartbreaking defeats, his mind was ever active, planning a new phase of the development of the kingdom of God in the last days: a temple in Kirtland, Zion, Nauvoo the Beautiful, a gathering place in the west, a thousand years of peace.

Joseph knew only one direction—that was forward. Joseph Smith at his death was still building Nauvoo into a major city of the West, devoting energy to a campaign for the presidency of the United States, and organizing explorers to seek out a location in the West where the Saints could move and become a mighty people.

Courage, remarkable courage—a visionary man, a creative and energetic man, an optimistic man, an enthusiastic man—how can you help but be impressed with someone who is irrespressible?

A leader, to be successful, must be courageous. Joseph asked his people to do nothing he would not do himself. Joseph Smith experienced life. The good and the bad literally came tumbling upon him from all directions. He met life and its experiences head-on with uncommon courage and literally absorbed all of it. On occasions he was taken back, but only momentarily, and then he was again surging forward as though he were searching, hungering for additional experiences. He relished life as few men have. All of his senses—physical, mental and spiritual—were so atuned that little was missed.

Joseph Smith had developed the attributes to prepare him to experience life to the fullest. He had developed an amazing spiritual capacity, remarkable physical body, a keen mind, and a delightful sense of humor.

By example he showed his people how to live.

Joseph Smith could not have succeeded if he had not had remarkable courage. Few have ever been faced with the fierce hate and determined opposition that Joseph faced. As great as his courage was, a courage that only a few have known, if it had been any less than it was, he would have failed.

Joseph Smith was completely unselfish. He gave of himself spiritually, intellectually, physically, and emotionally.

He was completely honest in all aspects of his personality. Joseph Smith honestly and openly expressed love. He honestly and openly expressed joy. He honestly and openly made public his weaknesses. He honestly and openly expressed his remorse. Contrary to the will of the Lord, Joseph Smith allowed Martin Harris to take the first 116 pages of the Book of Mormon manuscript that had been translated. Martin lost them, and the Lord chastized Joseph severely. Joseph made no attempt to hide his error or the Lord's rebuke. In fact, if one wants to read the account, it is in Sections three and ten of the Doctrine and Covenants—readily available for all the world to read. This tells us something about Joseph. He did not try to hide his weaknesses. His reason for such honesty was that he desired to show his people how to live, how to love, how to feel, and how to react. He was more concerned with helping another by example than he was with improving his own image or building his own ego.

Joseph Smith was concerned only with serving his Savior, Jesus Christ, just as Jesus was concerned only with serving his Father in Heaven. This attitude of Joseph's taking his work seriously but himself lightly permitted him an attitude of freedom, a relaxed condition. He could be himself; sometimes carefree, sometimes intense, sometimes sad, sometimes lifted up in spiritual ecstasy. There were many dimensions to his personality—always sensitive, always concerned, always seeking to assist, in some way to bless another.

The Prophet's cousin, George A. Smith, observed Joseph on the Zion's Camp march and wrote:

> The Prophet took a full share of the fatigues of the entire journey. In addition to the care of providing for the Camp and presiding over it, he walked most of the time and had a full proportion of blistered, bloody and sore feet, which was the natural result of walking from twenty-five to forty miles a day, in the hot season of the year.
>
> But during the entire trip he never uttered a murmur; while most of the men in the Camp complained to him of sore toes, blistered feet, long drives, scanty provisions, poor quality of bread, bad corn dodger, frowzy butter, strong honey, maggoty bacon and cheese, etc. Even a dog could not bark at some men without their murmuring at Joseph. If they had to camp with bad water, it nearly caused a rebellion. Yet we were the Camp of Zion, and many of us were prayerless, thoughtless, careless, heedless, foolish, or devilish, and we did not know it. Joseph had to bear with us and tutor us like children. There were many, however, in the Camp who never murmured and who were always ready and willing to do as our leaders desired.[1]

---

[1]Quoted in Evans, John Henry, *Joseph Smith, an American Prophet* (Salt Lake City: Deseret Book Co., 1966), pp. 117-18.

Young though he was, he was like a father to Saints of all ages—a wise father, a loving father, filled with wisdom.

Yes, Joseph was a worthy model then and today because he was selfless. He did not have time for petty thoughts. His mind was occupied with principles of salvation. The greatness of the thoughts crowded out self-pity, jealousy, meanness, and pride.

He knew the truth and the truth made him free—free from fear, free from doubt, free from pessimism. Joseph said:

If I were sunk in the lowest pit of Nova Scotia, with the Rocky Mountains piled on me, I would hang on, exercise faith, and keep up good courage, and I would come out on top.[2]

In a letter to John Smith the Prophet wrote:

. . . I wrote these few lines to inform you that we feel determined in this place not to be dismayed if hell boils over all at once. We feel to hope for the best, and determined to prepare for the worst.[3]

Joseph Smith could look any man in the eye. This gave him power. There was no pretense in Joseph Smith. He was what he was and grateful to the Lord for what God had brought him to be. The credit was to the Lord, and Joseph praised his name. Joseph Smith looked upon himself first as a servant of his Lord Jesus Christ, and this caused him to react to situations in a way which is unusual to the people of the world. Let us consider one example:

The Prophet's Astonishing Humility

The revelations came rapidly to Joseph Smith in the years 1829-31. They were important revelations. They were revelations pertaining to the establishment and governance of the kingdom of God restored to the earth. A conference was called in the latter part of 1831, and the brethren of the priesthood assembled in the home of John Johnson in Hiram, Ohio. The Prophet Joseph Smith presented to those assembled a number of revelations and asked them to consider them and approve of them as worthy of being published as a latter-day book of scripture

[2]Quoted in *Joseph Smith, an American Prophet*, p. 9.
[3]HC 6:485-86.

to be titled the Book of Commandments.[4] Those assembled quickly demonstrated that they had minds of their own, and in essence they confronted the twenty-five year old prophet with the challenge: "How do we know that the revelations are of God? The language sounds so very much like the language of Joseph Smith."

Here is an excellent opportunity to view historically another incident that gives insight to what Joseph Smith was like. He did not appear to be offended. He took the question in stride. I feel he was honestly perplexed. He knew the revelations were from God. I have wondered if he truly ever thought of why they sounded as they sounded. He did not become defensive. He did not rebuke them for questioning a prophet of God. But he very simply suggested an approach to the problem which he had utilized numerous times before. In essence his reply to the question was a candid "I don't know" followed by the words, "Let's ask the Lord." They knelt with him and he petitioned God for the answer. The answer was received in an effective, forceful, but most unpretentious way. No angel appeared; no audible voice was heard. The Prophet simply said to his scribe, "Please record the following." And then, speaking in measured sentences slow enough for a man to record the revelation in longhand, Joseph dictated the revelation as given to him by the Lord. But the answer sought is part of a comprehensive revelation of both warning and hope to the whole earth—a revelation which was to be known as the preface to the Book of Commandments and today is Section One of the Doctrine and Covenants. Verses 24–27 are the verses that directly answer the question Joseph asked of God:

Behold, I am God and have spoken it; these commandments are of me, and were given unto my servants in their weakness, after the manner of their language, that they might come to understanding.

And inasmuch as they erred it might be made known;

And inasmuch as they sought wisdom they might be instructed;

[4]From a consideration of incomplete historical records, following is what I believe took place relative to the presentation of a new book of scripture and its ultimate acceptance. See also William E. Berrett, *Teachings of the Doctrine and Covenants* (Salt Lake City: Deseret Book Co., 1961) pp. 2-6.

And inasmuch as they sinned they might be chastened, that they might repent. . . .

One would think that this amazing demonstration of the receiving of such a reasonable and satisfying answer would have silenced his questioners. But it did not, at least not all. William E. McLellan had had more formal education than any of the others. He was an impressive man. He continued to question Joseph. Again the Prophet sought the help of God. The revelation he received is a classic example of the principle stated by the Lord in the first revelation given that day to his servant. The Lord is interested in communicating with his children so they can understand and, if necessary, change their ways. The second revelation of the day is also in the Doctrine and Covenants and says rather simply:

Your eyes have been upon my servant Joseph Smith, Jun., and his language you have known; and his imperfections you have known; and you have sought in your hearts knowledge that you might express beyond his language; this you also know.

Now, seek ye out of the Book of Commandments, even the least that is among them, and appoint him that is the most wise among you;

Or, if there be any among you that shall make one like unto it, then ye are justified in saying that ye do not know that they are true;

But if ye cannot make one like unto it, ye are under condemnation if ye do not bear record that they are true.[5]

William E. McLellan was selected as being, by the standards of the world, the wisest in the group, and his assignment was to write a revelation that would sound as good and make a contribution equal to the "least" revelation presented by Joseph Smith. Brother McLellan was a complete failure; he could not write anything that sounded like a revelation. The next day he manifested an attitude of meekness as he offered his sustaining vote and his apologies to the youthful prophet. Now, with the approval of the body of the priesthood, plans were quickly made and put into action for the publication of the new book of scripture.

[5]D&C 67:5-8.

Mob intervention delayed the publication of the book. By the time publication could be resumed, additional revelations had been received, and it was determined that a new title, "The Doctrine and Covenants," would be more descriptive of the volume of modern day scripture. Joseph Smith's humility in the foregoing situation is astonishing. His humble attitude is further reflected in a letter written by Joseph to the members of the Quorum of the Twelve while they were laboring in England.

How pleasing it is for brethren to dwell together in unity. Let the Saints of the Most High ever cultivate this principle, and the most glorious blessings must result, not only to them individually, but to the whole Church. . . .

. . . *There are many things of much importance, on which you ask counsel, but which I think you will be perfectly able to decide upon, as you are more conversant with the peculiar circumstances than I am; and I feel great confidence in your united wisdom;* therefore you will excuse me for not entering into detail. If I should see anything that is wrong, I would take the privilege of making known my mind to you, and pointing out the evil. (Italics added.)

Beloved brethren, you must be aware in some measure of my feelings, when I contemplate the great work which is now rolling on, and the relationship which I sustain to it, while it is extending to distant lands, and thousands are embracing it. I realize in some measure my responsibility, and the need I have of support from above, and wisdom from on high, that I may be able to teach this people, which have now become a great people, the principles of righteousness, and lead them agreeably to the will of Heaven; so that they may be perfected, and prepared to meet the Lord Jesus Christ when He shall appear in great glory. *Can I rely on your prayers to our Heavenly Father on my behalf, and on all the prayers of all my brethren and sisters in England, (Whom having not seen, yet I love)*, that I may be enabled to escape every strategem of Satan, surmount every difficulty, and bring this people to the enjoyment of those blessings which are reserved for the righteous? I ask this at your hands in the name of the Lord Jesus Christ. (Italics added.)

In conclusion the Prophet says:

. . . Let every selfish feeling be not only buried, but annihilated; and let love to God and man predominate. . . .

Let us realize that we are not to live to ourselves, but to God; by so doing the greatest blessing will rest upon us both in time and in eternity.

. . . Give my love to all the brethren and sisters and tell them I should have been pleased to come over to England to see them, but I am afraid that I shall be under necessity of remaining here for some time; therefore I give them a pressing invitation to come and see me.

I remain, dear brethren, yours affectionately,

JOSEPH SMITH[6]

Joseph Smith's submissive nature permitted him to enjoy the companionship of the Spirit of the Lord and the resultant blessing of such a companionship.

A Voice of Gladness

One would expect, and almost rightly so, that with so much adversity Joseph would almost always be sober, serious, and perhaps overly pious. This might be expected, but it was not the case.

Joseph did not fit the stereotype, the usual image of a prophet. He was a large, muscular young man who loved athletics and had a keen sense of humor. He was an impressive, memorable individual. Brigham Young said, years later: "I feel like shouting hallelujah all the time when I think I ever knew Joseph Smith the Prophet."[7] Joseph's balance, his perspective, his enthusiasm in the face of opposition and tragedy were remarkable. He acted and reacted in a manner which was peculiar to himself. He did not confine his behavior to that which was conventional, nor to that which was expected by society.

Parley P. Pratt wrote a vivid description of Joseph Smith and among other things emphasized the fact that Joseph Smith was "affable, had an unconscious smile and was cheerful."

President Joseph Smith was in person tall and well built, strong and active; of a light complexion, light hair, blue eyes, very little beard, and of an expression peculiar to himself, on which the eye naturally rested with interest, and was never weary of beholding. His countenance was ever mild, affable, beaming with intelligence and benevolence; mingled with a look of interest and an unconscious

---

[6]HC 4:226-32.
[7]JD 3:511.

smile, or cheerfulness, and entirely free from all restraint or affectation of gravity; and there was something connected with the serene and steady penetrating glance of his eye, as if he would penetrate the deepest abyss of the human heart, gaze into eternity, penetrate the heavens, and comprehend all worlds.[8]

Among other things, a St. Louis reporter wrote:

. . . The Prophet's most remarkable feature is his eye. . . . His voice is low and soft and his smile, which is frequent, is agreeable.[9]

The fact that Joseph loved athletics and often relaxed by engaging in athletic contests is evident from entries in his journal such as the following:

Played ball with the Brethren a short time.[10]

I wrestled with William Wall, the most expert wrestler in Ramus, and threw him.[11]

Rode out in the afternoon . . . and afterwards played ball with the boys.[12]

Why was Joseph able to be cheerful, hopeful, pleasant, and engage in fun-filled activities? I think his own pen reveals the reason:

Now, what do we hear in the gospel which we have received? A voice of gladness! A voice of mercy from heaven; and a voice of truth out of the earth; glad tidings for the dead; a voice of gladness for the living and the dead; glad tidings of great joy. How beautiful upon the mountains are the feet of those that bring glad tidings of good things, that say unto Zion: Behold, thy God reigneth! As the dews of Carmel, so shall the knowledge of God descend upon them!

And again, what do we hear? Glad tidings from Cumorah! Moroni, an angel from heaven, declaring the fulfillment of the prophets—the book to be revealed. A voice of the Lord in the wilderness of Fayette, Seneca county, declaring the three witnesses to bear record of the book!

Brethren, shall we not go on in so great a cause? Go forward and not backward. Courage, brethren; and on, on to the victory! Let your hearts rejoice and be exceedingly glad. Let the earth break forth into singing. Let the dead speak forth anthems of eternal praise to the King Immanuel. . . .

---

[8]*Pratt*, pp. 45-46.
[9]*Evans*, pp. 178-79.
[10]HC 5:260.
[11]*Ibid.*, p. 302.
[12]*Ibid.*, p. 307.

Let the mountains shout for joy, and all ye valleys cry aloud; and all ye seas and dry lands tell the wonders of your Eternal King; And ye rivers and brooks, and rills, flow down with gladness. Let the woods and all the trees of the field praise the Lord; and ye solid rocks weep for joy! And let the sun, moon, and the morning stars sing together, and let all the sons of God shout for joy. And let the eternal creations declare his name forever and ever.[13]

Perhaps it would be well for us who also on occasion have difficult decisions to make and have burdens to bear and occasionally have sorrow come uninvited into our lives—perhaps we should consider that which permitted Joseph to be cheerful, optimistic, and joyful. He had eternal perspective. He had viewed the eternal worlds and had seen the eternal possibilities of the patient, faithful person. He knew with certainty the reality of God and His Son. He knew the necessary price had been paid for our sins, and that through obedience we could dwell with God. That knowledge filled him with joy. Through the revelations of God to Joseph, and through his writings and teachings, we may also know and be filled with joy. How unfortunate that on occasions we lose sight and perspective of our eternal opportunities and, as a result, experience unhappiness. Joseph wrote the following concerning the purpose of our existence:

Happiness is the object and design of our existence; and will be the end thereof, if we pursue the path that leads to it; and this path is virtue, uprightness, faithfulness, holiness, and keeping all the commandments of God.[14]

The Prophet knew that happiness was not necessarily the by-product of an undisturbed life—that happiness did not necessarily come because of the absence of difficulties. Rather, happiness is the result of a commitment to the Lord Jesus Christ and the privilege of being a recipient of the Holy Spirit, which brings peace, hope, and joy. This knowledge is not secret; it is attested to in the scriptures and in the teachings of prophets of God. But sometimes the reality of this truth is obscured by false philosophies and the enticements of the

---

[13]D&C 128:19, 20, 22, 23.
[14]HC 5:134-35.

world. Some have the idea that the truly religious life is dull, drab, uninteresting. It would be difficult to find anything dull, drab, or uninteresting in the life of Joseph, the Prophet. His life from the beginning to end was literally crowded with excitment and challenge. The Lord does not direct his servants to the periphery but to the forefront of the battle of life. Everyone who truly wants to follow the Lord and Savior Jesus Christ will find a most interesting, meaningful, vital life. If the follower of Jesus will permit the intercession of the Holy Spirit into his personal life, that follower will immediately discover that his life will not be wasted in a meaningless expenditure of energy. The servant of God will be directed to participate in that which is truly meaningful—not meaningful by the consensus of a group or a committee, but meaningful by the witness of God who is the possessor of all knowledge. Happiness, it would seem, would almost of necessity have to result from a sure knowledge that one is engaged in something of importance to God, his fellowmen, and himself. It would also follow that such a person would have confidence in himself and have purpose in his life. Joseph Smith is a remarkable example of one who captured those things of most importance in life.

Thy Will and Not Mine Be Done

The greatness of Joseph Smith was his greatness as a follower of the Lord Jesus Christ. Joseph Smith, following in the footsteps of his Savior, Jesus Christ, learned the meaning of persecution. Joseph experienced the blind, irrational behavior of some ignorant human beings. He knew what it was to be hurt again and again by unkind remarks. He knew the feeling of being laughed at, ridiculed, and insulted. He knew the discomfort of physical abuse and the unfairness of corrupt public officials. It seems apparent that these continual adverse experiences increased the Prophet's awareness of the feelings and needs of his fellow human beings. He appreciated deeply any display of kindness or any word of encouragement. While in the Liberty Jail, he thanked Mrs. Norman Bull for visiting him and said of his imprisonment: "It seems to me that my heart will always be more tender after this experience that it ever before."[15] On another occasion he said, "God does not look on sin with allowance, but when men have sinned, there must be allowance made for them."[16] To the members of the Relief Society he cautioned:

I have one request to make of the President and members of the society, that you search yourselves—the tongue is an unruly member—hold your tongues about things of no moment.

. . . Put a double watch over the tongue. . . . The object is to make those not so good reform and return to the path of virtue that they may be numbered with the good. . . .[17]

Joseph Smith was given great responsibility in life, responsibility that brought him in contact with mean and vile people—people who often showed no mercy. This treatment did not deaden the Prophet's sensitivity to good and right, but increased it.

The power of God was in Joseph Smith, the surging power that can come only to a man who has faith in the Lord Jesus Christ and has proven his devotion in the fires of adversity.

George Q. Cannon said of Joseph Smith:

Think of what he passed through! Think of his afflictions, and think of his dauntless character! Did any one ever see any lack in him of the power necessary to enable thim to stand with dignity in the midst of his enemies, or lacking in dignity in the performance of his duties as a servant of the living God? God gave him peculiar power in this respect. He was filled with integrity to God; with such integrity as was not known among men. He was like an angel of God among them. Notwithstanding all that he had to endure, and the peculiar circumstances in which he was so often placed, the great responsibility that weighed constantly upon him, he never faltered; the feeling of fear or trembling never crossed him—at least he never exhibited it in his feelings or actions. God sustained him to the very last, and was with him and bore him off triumphant even in his death.[18]

---

[15]*Ibid.*, 6:286.
[16]*Ibid.*, 5:24.
[17]*Ibid.*, p. 20.
[18]*JD* 23:362.

Joseph never let the Lord down and faltered rarely and only momentarily. Joseph bore witness of God under the most trying and dangerous circumstances and did the work of the Lord when it literally cost him tears, sweat, and blood. Joseph Smith would translate when his body cried out for food; the voice of his great spirit cried out stronger for knowledge and truth. His dedication, proven in several states, was not to go unrewarded. When Joseph Smith stepped into the presence of a man, that man knew that here was a representative of God. When Joseph Smith stood before a congregation, his muscular body pulsed with the spirit of God and his eyes penetrated the very souls of those who sat before him—friends and enemies.

People speak of greatness of Joseph Smith. What greatness? The greatness of a prophet, an intellectual, a leader of men, a husband and father, a son, a humanitarian—yes, all of these. But his true greatness lies in his relationship with his God.

Joseph Smith, the representative of Jesus Christ, whose reaction from the first time he knelt in the grove of trees as a boy not yet fourteen years of age until he died a martyr by a mobster's bullet when he was not yet thirty-nine years of age, was "Thy will and not mine be done."

He did not enjoy persecution. He did not enjoy bearing burdens alone. He did not enjoy suffering, his own suffering or the suffering of loved ones. He did not enjoy privation, hunger, or hardship. He did not want to die. He had a relish for life. He cherished it perhaps as few men have. He did not want to leave his farm, his city, his wife, his unborn child. But Joseph's response to all of this was "not my will, but thy will be done."

6 THE ROLE OF A PROPHET

A Spokesman for the Lord

Moses said, "I will now turn aside and see this great sight,"[1] and he approached a burning bush which was not being consumed. God spoke to him, "Put off thy shoes from thy feet, for the place whereon thou standest is holy ground".[2]

Moses, though reluctant, was called to be a prophet. When Moses protested because of his weaknesses, the Lord said, "Now therefore go, and I will be with thy mouth, and teach thee what thou shalt say".[3] Moses was still hesitant, and the Lord agreed to give him his brother Aaron as a spokesman. The Lord said Moses would be to Aaron as God was to Moses. That is, Aaron would speak only what the Lord told him to speak.[4] The Lord leaves no question as to the role of a prophet. He is directed by God, and he is God's spokesman on the earth and is responsible to God. Speaking on this subject, Brigham Young said:

> I was speaking about this matter last night, about the feelings of the people towards the Prophet Joseph. The mass of the people never realized, to the day of his death, but what Joseph was made by them. They actually believed that he was amenable to the people, that he did not know it all, and that other men knew things which he did not know concerning the Kingdom of God on the earth. . . .

[1]Exodus 3:3.
[2]Exodus 3:5.
[3]Exodus 4:12.
[4]Exodus 4:15-16.

As I have already observed, comparatively few learned, in the days of Joseph, that he was placed between the people and God, and that they had no more right to dictate him than they had to dictate the angel Gabriel, that they had no more business to interfere with him, or call him to an account, than we have to call to an account the angel Gabriel.[5]

A prophet is a teacher of eternal truths. He is an example of righteousness, a condemner of wickedness, a forseer of the future, and an inspired leader of men.

Two Kinds of Men on the Earth

A battle was waged in heaven to guarantee that God's children when they came to this earth would have individual moral free agency. He who would have taken that away was cast from heaven with his followers, and those who followed the plan of the Lord Jesus Christ wept for them.

The children of God on this earth may select good or evil, and often the selection effects more than just the individual. An example is Moroni, that great military leader spoken of in Alma in the Book of Mormon:

And Moroni was a strong and mighty man; he was a man of a perfect understanding . . . if all men had been, and were, and ever would be, like unto Moroni, behold, the very powers of hell would have been shaken forever; yea, the devil would never have power over the hearts of the children of men.[6]

Amalickiah, on the other hand, brought sorrow, destruction, and death to two nations because of his desire to do extreme wickedness. The Book of Mormon says of him:

Yea, and also see the great wickedness one very wicked man can cause to take place among the children of men. Yea we see that Amalickiah, because he was a man of cunning device and a man of many flattering words, that he led away the hearts of many people to do wickedly. . . .[7]

In Joseph Smith's day there were both kinds of men—righteous and evil. Joseph Smith was blessed with many friends

---

[5]JD 3:318.
[6]Alma 48:11, 17.
[7]Alma 46:9, 10.

and associates who elected to do good and to be faithful and loyal supporters. Numerous people have testified of the goodness of the Prophet of the last dispensation by their works. Word tributes are needful, but a testimony of deeds is preferable. Many followers of Joseph bore eloquent testimony of him and the God he represented and the gospel he espoused by their actions.

Faithful Followers of the Prophet

At the height of bitter apostasy in Kirtland, Ohio, in 1837, Joseph Smith and Heber C. Kimball were sitting near the sacrament table in the Kirtland Temple, and the Prophet said: "The Lord has whispered, let my servant Heber open the door of the Gospel to the people of England." Heber C. Kimball was stunned and replied, "Can Brother Brigham go with me?" "No," the Prophet replied, "the Lord has other work for Brigham."[8] The Prophet was asking much of Heber. Heber was convinced that Joseph spoke for God. He would be required to leave his family in a near destitute condition. He laid his hands upon his wife and then each of the children in turn and invoked God to care for them. He wept as he blessed them. Later Heber recalled his assignment to England:

I have seen the day when it was as much as our lives were worth to sustain Joseph Smith—the apostates were so thick around us, and persecution was so great.

Brigham said, "Go, brother Heber, and in the name of Israel's God you shall be blessed, and it shall prove the salvation of thousands."

John Boynton, one of the Twelve, came to me and said, "If you are such a damned fool as to listen to Joseph Smith, the fallen Prophet, and go to England under these perilous circumstances, if I knew you were shipwrecked on Van Dieman's Land I would not assist you to get you from that land."

I will speak to Lyman Johnson's credit: I will give every man credit for the good he does. Lyman Johnson steps up and says, "Brother Heber, I do not feel so. I am sorry you are going, and consider you are foolish; but if you are determined to go, I will

---

[8]See Whitney, pp. 120-21.

help you all that is in my power; and he took from his shoulders a good, nice camlet cloak and put it on to mine; and that was the first cloak I ever had.

Those circumstances were the most trying circumstances that ever I was brought into. Joseph had to flee from that land to save his body from being slain, and so had brother Brigham and every other man who would sustain the Prophet, the apostasy was so great; and they were most hellish in their wickedness.

I went and performed the mission according to the words of the Prophet of the Living God. . . . God had blessed and prospered me exceedingly, and the words of Joseph and Brigham were all fulfilled to the letter. . . .[9]

Heber C. Kimball was permitted to stay in England for only eight months, and then he was needed at home by his leader, Joseph Smith. He had baptized 1,500 people in those eight months. He described the scene and his feelings as he bid farewell to those in England who had come into the kingdom of God. Children took hold of his hand or coat and wept. Parents stood by the door or leaned out of the windows and called out their goodbyes. They said, "Oh how can we get along without our dear Elder Kimball." And Heber said, "As I left them and walked along the country road, I wept and I went to the stream of water three times to bathe my eyes"; and he records, "I thought mine eyes were a fountain of tears."[10]

He performed his mission "according to the words of the Prophet of the living God," and what a mission it was! It seems that part of the cost of success in the Lord's work is a willingness to serve when it is inconvenient.

Joseph had learned this lesson and learned it well, and gave his associates the opportunity to learn the important lesson for themselves. Never again would Heber C. Kimball be the same Heber C. Kimball; at the cost of personal sacrifice for a higher cause, his soul had been enlarged, his capacity increased, and his faith strengthened beyond that which it had been. Heber C. Kimball would never falter as a servant of God. Joseph

[9]JD 6:65.
[10]Whitney, p. 206.

Smith not only had the capacity to serve the Lord himself, but he had the capacity to help create dedicated servants.

The Prophet Joseph Smith prophesied on July 4, 1838, in Far West, that on that same day one year later, the Quorum of the Twelve would take leave from Far West. Brigham Young, by his own admission had, since his removal to Kirtland in 1832, stayed by the Prophet Joseph Smith, studied him, and attempted to emulate him. Brigham Young's behavior in 1839 during the Prophet's imprisonment certainly did credit to the name of Joseph Smith. Far West was in the hands of bitter enemies in 1839, but Brigham Young would not have a prophecy of Joseph Smith's go unfulfilled. At the peril of his own life and the lives of those who travelled with him, he returned to Far West to fulfill the prophecy. They literally infiltrated enemy lines, held a meeting at the temple site, and took leave for their mission. There were some who protested that it was not reasonable. It was not expected, it was difficult to do, it was too inconvenient.

The faithful apostles returned to Nauvoo. Prior to their departure to England, they were overcome by illness and postponed leaving. As weeks passed, it became obvious that when the Lord called them through his servant Joseph, no "conditions" had been placed on that call. They were to go whether well or ill. When Brigham Young, who lived in Montrose, Iowa, started on his mission, he was assisted into a boat and crossed the river to Nauvoo. He was so weak that he could not walk the short distance to Heber C. Kimball's house, but lay by the river until Israel Barlow came along and helped him onto his horse and took him to Heber's house. Heber was also ill, as were nearly all the members of his family. Prior to the day of their departure, Mary Ann Young, Brigham's wife, came to be with him. On the appointed day of their departure, they were assisted into a wagon. Their wives were ill with fever, and both were in bed. Also both had given birth to babies within the previous two weeks! Heber recorded the farewell as follows:

It was with difficulty we got into the wagon, and started down the hill about ten rods; it appeared to me as though my very inmost parts would melt within me at leaving my family in such a condition, as it were almost in the arms of death. I felt as though I could not endure it. I asked the Teamster to stop, and said to Brother Brigham, "This is pretty tough, isn't it; let's rise up and give them a cheer." We arose, and swinging our hats three times over our heads, shouted: "Hurrah, hurrah for Israel." Vilate, hearing the noise, arose from her bed and came to the door. She had a smile on her face. Vilate and Mary Ann Young cried out to us: "Good bye, God bless you." We returned the compliment, and then told the driver to go ahead. After this I felt a spirit of joy and gratitude, having had the satisfaction of seeing my wife standing upon her feet, intead of leaving her in bed, knowing well that I should not see them again for two or three years.[11]

At approximately this same time Wilford Woodruff departed for his mission. He was suffering from chills and fever, and he was so weak that he had to rest after only walking to the Nauvoo post office. Joseph Smith came by and gave him some "parting advice" and bade him farewell.

Wilford Woodruff, referring to this incident, makes an interesting observation concerning the Prophet Joseph. ". . . His demeanor in parting was something that I had never noticed or experienced before."[12] He does not explain his observation of the Prophet, but the Prophet must have had deep feelings of empathy and sympathy seeing his brethren depart in such difficult circumstance, though he knew that it must be so.

Inconvenient Service Continuing Example

Today advertisements in brilliant color on television and in magazines attempt to persuade us that we owe it to ourselves to have more and more conveniences. I am certain that all of us desire, and in many cases it would be desirable for us, to be able to accomplish routine tasks in life with less difficulty and with less expenditure of time. I am especially certain that all of us are pleased to travel by automobile or airplane rather than by horseback or carriage. I am certain that we like to turn a thermostat to heat our home rather than carry in wood by the

---

[11]*Ibid.*, p. 276.
[12]JD 24:53.

armload and coal by the bucketfull. We like to touch a switch
to light the house, and vacuum instead of sweeping the floors—
conveniences, good, worthy, helpful conveniences!

But with all these things we must be on guard that we as
individuals do not respond only when it is convenient. The
Lord has always insisted that his disciples serve not just when
it was convenient, but even when it was most inconvenient.
Joseph Smith exemplified that spirit of service from that spring
day in 1820 until that June day in 1844. This kind of dedication
he also requested of others who followed the Lord Jesus Christ;
and they most often, struggling to exercise faith which would
match the Prophet Joseph's, responded even when they were in
the most trying of circumstances. We will note that as we turn
the pages of Church history from that date (1839) forward,
the names Brigham Young, Heber C. Kimball, and Wilford
Woodruff appear many times. As we read these same Church
history books, the names of those members of the Twelve who
found it too inconvenient to return to Far West or to go to
England are conspicuous only by their complete absence. The
principle taught by the words and deeds of Joseph Smith all
his life is also in great evidence among his followers today.
Though the passing years have brought great conveniences in
our way of life, we ourselves have learned that today, as in all
days past, we serve our Lord even when it is inconvenient.

The Great Cost of Disloyalty

Joseph Smith had many worthy, dedicated followers
who lightened his burden; but, on the other hand, Joseph's
life was made more difficult, and he had to endure much
hardship and suffering, because of those who had made
covenants at baptism that they would bear his and the other
Saint's burdens, and then did not live up to those covenants.

Brigham Young said:

There are many witnesses here, not only witnesses of Joseph
and his career, but witnesses of the disaffected spirits that have
come into this Church and gone out again. Are there witnesses of

men trying to rise up and usurp Joseph's place in his day? Yes, there are many witnesses, that many men tried it. Are there witnesses here, of the rise and fall of men in this kingdom? Yes plenty of them. I have witnessed more than has been pleasing to me. It delights me to see men come into the Church and magnify the holy Priesthood, but it is a grievious matter to see men turn away from the whole commandments delivered unto them.

Let me ask this congregation, that portion of it that was in Jackson County; and again that portion that was in Kirtland in the days of Joseph, and in leaving Kirtland; and then those that were in Caldwell and Davis counties, Missouri; then ask those who were in Nauvoo in his day, and after he was slain; these portions of my congregation which I have mentioned, I will ask, what has produced your persecutions and sorrow? *What has been the starting point of all your afflictions? They began with apostates in your midst; these disaffected spirits caused others to come in, worse than they. . . .*

That has been the starting point and grand cause of all our difficulties, every time we were driven. Are there not witnesses of this, here? Yes, a good portion of this congregation are witnesses of these things.[13] (Italics added.)

As one reads the list of early Church leaders, the intimate friends and associates of Joseph Smith, it is astonishing how many were disloyal to the Prophet and either permanently left the Church or left it on a temporary basis.

Each of the three witnesses left: Martin Harris, friend and benefactor of Joseph Smith; Oliver Cowdery, who wrote almost the entire Book of Mormon as Joseph dictated it—assistant president of the Church, capable, intelligent, scholarly Oliver—lost in apostasy; David Whitmer, who with Joseph and Oliver beheld an angel holding the plates and heard the voice of God speaking from the heavens. David Whitmer and Joseph Smith had resided in the same home for months. To have any one of these three personal friends, fellow witnesses, leave the faith and reject Joseph's prophetic calling would have been distressing, but how difficult to lose all three. Of the eight witnesses, half apostatized; some became very vocal in renouncing Joseph Smith. As one glances through the names of the original Quorum of the Twelve selected in 1835, no less

---
[13]*Ibid.*, 1:82.

than half apostatized. Some left briefly and then returned repentant; some were never to return. Wilford Woodruff, speaking of this apostasy, said:

I passed through that scene [great apostasy in Kirtland], as did some others who are now with us. . . . Even Apostles took occasion to rise up and endeavored to dictate and direct the Prophet of God. Those who testified to the Book of Mormon were led away through not keeping the commandments of God and thinking that they themselves were great men. Some of them were learned men; some of them considered themselves very smart men, and they were so smart that they wanted to dictate and direct the Prophet of God. The consequence of all this was that they turned aside from the commandments of God. Some of them had been true and faithful in their labors in the ministry. I have heard Oliver Cowdery testify of the Book of Mormon by the power of God, when it seemed as if the very earth trembled under his feet. He was filled with the Holy Ghost and the power of God while he was faithful, and so were many of these men. But Oliver Cowdery yielded to the temptation of the evil one, and we may say he apostatized. So did Martin Harris, and several others connected with them. They left the Church, they turned against Joseph and they said he was a fallen prophet, and they themselves wanted to direct the Church. Several of these men called upon me in that time of apostasy and asked me to join them against the Prophet; the Prophet was fallen, they said. Now, I had seen enough myself of the Prophet of God and I had read enough of the revelations of God through him, to know that he was a Prophet of God, and not a fallen Prophet. I saw that these men were yielding to the devil, and I told them so. Said I: "You will all go to hell unless you repent. Joseph has been raised up by the power of God and to the Church and kingdom of God here on the earth."[14]

Joseph Smith knew the danger was not from designated enemies but so-called friends. At a meeting of the city council in December, 1843, the subject of the menace to the city and the mayor was under consideration, and Joseph said among other things:

. . . I am exposed to far greater danger from traitors among ourselves than from enemies without, although my life has been sought for many years by the civil and military authorities, priests and

---

[14]Doxey, Roy W., *The Latter-day Prophets and the Doctrine and Covenants,* (Salt Lake City: Deseret Book Co.) 4:214-15.

people of Missouri; and if I can escape from the ungrateful treachery of assassins, I can live as Caesar might have lived, were it not for a right-hand Brutus. I have pretended friends betray me. All the enemies upon the face of the earth may roar and exert all their power to bring about my death, but they can accomplish nothing, unless some who are among us, who have enjoyed our society, have been with us in our councils, participated in our confidence, taken us by the hand, called us brother, saluted us with a kiss, join with our enemies, turn our virtues into faults, and, by falsehood and deceit, stir up their wrath and indignation against us, and bring their united vengeance upon our heads. All the hue and cry of the chief priests and elders against the Savior could not bring down the wrath of the Jewish nation upon his head, and thereby cause the crucifixion of the Son of God, until Judas said unto them, "Whomsoever I shall kiss he is the man; hold him fast." Judas was one of the Twelve Apostles, even their treasurer, and dipped with their Master in the dish, and through his treachery, the crucifixion was brought about, and *we have a Judas in our midst*.[15] (Italics added.)

It would be surprising to find a prophet who was without opposition. Joseph Smith, at age seventeen, was informed that he would not escape it. He was told that his name would be known throughout the world for good and also for evil.

On this subject, Brigham Young said:

I never preached to the world but what the cry was, "That damned old Joe Smith has done thus and so. I would tell the people that they did not know him, and I did, and that I knew him to be a good man; and that when they spoke against him, they spoke against as good a man as ever lived.

I wish you all to understand that no Elders go to any place among the world, but what the wicked find fault with the people of God. They found fault with Joseph Smith, and at length killed him, as they have a great many others of the Latter-day Saints. What for? Because of his wickedness? No. But the cry was, "Away with him, we cannot do with this man nor with his people." Did they hate him for his evil works? No. If he had been a liar, a swearer, a gambler, or in any way an evil doer, and of the world, it would have loved its own, and they would have embraced him, and nourished and kept him. If he had been a false prophet they never would have lifted a hand against him, because he could have spread still more delusion through the world around him.[16]

---

[15]HC 6:152.
[16]JD 4:77-78.

Had It Been an Enemy, We Could Have Borne It

The loss of friends hurt Joseph deeply, and when he learned in Nauvoo of a secret plot to overthrow him, he wept. We get insight into the Prophet's poignant feelings by reading the following letter written to W. W. Phelps, who had been in apostasy and had written to the Prophet to ask forgiveness and to be reinstated into the Church. Brother Phelps's defection had hurt Joseph deeply:

Dear Brother Phelps:—I must say that it is with no ordinary feelings I endeavor to write a few lines to you. I am rejoiced at the privilege granted me.

You may in some measure realize my feelings, as well as Elder Rigdon's and Brother Hyrum's, when we read your letter—truly our hearts were melted into tenderness and compassion when we ascertained your resolves, and etc. I can assure you I feel a disposition to act on your case in a manner that will meet the approbation of Jehovah (whose servant I am), and agreeable to the principles of truth and righteousness which have been revealed; and inasmuch as long-suffering, patience, and mercy have ever characterized the dealings of our Heavenly Father towards the humble and penitent, I feel disposed to copy the example, cherish the same principles, and by so doing be a savior of my fellow men.

It is true, that we have suffered much in consequence of your behavior—the cup of gall, already full enough for mortals to drink, was indeed filled to overflowing when you turned against us. One with whom we had oft taken sweet counsel together, and enjoyed many refreshing seasons from the Lord—*"Had it be an enemy, we could have borne it"* . . . however, the cup has been drunk. . . . (Italics added.)

Believing your confession to be real, and your repentance genuine, I shall be happy once again to give you the right hand of fellowship, and rejoice over the returning prodigal.

Your letter was read to the Saints last Sunday, and an expression of their feeling was taken, when it was unanimously, RESOLVED, that W. W. Phelps should be received into fellowship.

"Come on, dear brother, since the war is past,
For Friends at first, are friends at last."

Yours as ever,

JOSEPH SMITH, JUN.[17]

---

[17]HC 4:162-64.

The Mouthpiece of the Almighty

It hurts to take action against one's friends and members of one's own family, but when action must be taken there can be no hesitancy. This is part of the role of a prophet.

The Prophet Joseph, imprisoned, wrote:

No power or influence can or ought to be maintained by virtue of the priesthood, only by persuasion, by long-suffering, by gentleness and meekness, and by love unfeigned;

By kindness, and pure knowledge, which shall greatly enlarge the soul without hypocrisy and without guile. . . .[18]

Regardless of circumstances, the prophet must lead, must maintain authority. He has no choice in this because he has been called by the Lord. On occasions the task at hand is so monumental that even with the utilization of all the excellent qualities described in the preceeding scripture, there may still remain a difficult problem, the solving of which will hurt some and offend others. It may even stir up anger, resentment, and bitterness. But the responsibility to move forward is still there. The weak leader will hedge, postpone, procrastinate and compromise; the strong leader, one who follows the spirit of the Lord, will do what is right and accept the consequences. Joseph Smith was a strong leader. After the exercise of all good and kind principles, problems still remained; and still, for the sake of the kingdom of God, action—difficult, heartbreaking action—had to be taken. Joseph Smith, as much as any man who has lived, knew well the responsibility that comes when one has God's authority upon him. How courageously he exercised it! Joseph was the one who held the keys, all the keys. He was the one who had to act. Others, his counselors and associates, could plead for more time, a less drastic course; but Joseph, as the leader, could not afford the luxury of procrastination, nor misplaced mercy, nor the idle hope that a situation might right itself in some unforseen way if no action at all were taken. Brigham Young said, on the subject:

Joseph Smith . . . was the mouthpiece of the Almighty, and was always ready to rebuke them when requisite. You who were ac-

[18]D&C 121:41-42.

quainted with him know his course and life. He had a word of comfort and consolation to the humble and faithful, and a word of rebuke to the forward and disobedient.[19]

Heartbreak, Yes—Compromise, No

Joseph Smith, the very teacher of gentleness and long suffering, often found that bold action was necessary. His close friend and advisor, Frederick G. Williams (the Prophet had named one of his sons for him), had to be removed from his place as a member of the First Presidency. Sidney Rigdon, first counselor to Joseph Smith, knowledgeable and articulate— yet Joseph could not afford to let sentiment for the past blur the reality of the present nor obstruct the vision of the future. How painful it must have been to recommend to the Saints congregated in conference in 1844 that the venerable old gentleman, the pillar of strength of the past—President Sidney Rigdon, whose name was almost synonymous with the restored gospel—must now be removed from his place. Others could allow mercy to overcome judgment and justice, but not the Prophet, Seer, and Revelator. The people overwhelmingly voted to reject Joseph Smith's counsel and voted to retain Sidney Rigdon. Many must have felt they did the right thing. After all, kindness and mercy are teachings of the Savior. But they were wrong, their assumptions were false, and their reasoning was incorrect. They had not supported their Prophet, and he was called and inspired of God. Gone was the opportunity to strengthen Joseph in a time when strength was most important. How much, just how much does a strong counselor mean to a president? How much did Heber C. Kimball mean to Brigham Young? Joseph pleaded, "Remove the weak, give me strength," but the plea fell on unresponsive ears. There were too many who felt that compassion at any time, at any price, was a virtue. They were wrong. Hurt—of course Joseph was hurt; he had been hurt before, and he would be hurt again.

Members of the Prophet's own family hurt him. His brother William accused Joseph of a lack of feeling because in

---

[19]JD 8:189.

a high council hearing he rejected his own mother's testimony because it was out of place. Joseph would take the abuse of members of his own family rather than compromise. The Prophet records the hurtful incident as follows:

> After supper I went to the High Council in company with my wife and some others that belonged to my household. I was solicited to take a seat with the Presidency and preside on a trial of Sister Elliot. I did so. My mother was called upon for testimony, and began to relate circumstances that had been brought before the Church and settled. I objected to such testimony. The complainant, Brother William Smith, arose and accused me of invalidating or doubting my Mother's testimony, which I had not done, nor did I desire to do so. I told him he was out of order, and asked him to sit down. He refused. I repeated my request. He became enraged. I finally ordered him to sit down. . . . I joined Brother Hyrum in trying to calm his stormy feelings, but to no purpose, he insisted that we intended to add abuse to injury, his passion increased, he arose abruptly, declared that he wanted no more to do with us. He rushed out at the door. We tried to prevail on him to stop, but all to no purpose. . . . He went home and spread the leaven of iniquity among my brothers, and especially prejudiced the mind of Brother Samuel. I soon learned that he was in the street exclaiming against me, and no doubt our enemies rejoiced at it. And where the matter will end I know not, but pray God to forgive him and them, and give them humility and repentance.
>
> The feelings of my heart I cannot express on this occasion, I can only pray to my Heavenly Father to open their eyes, that they may discover where they stand, that they may extricate themselves from the snare they have fallen into.[20]

How hard it is to be misunderstood by the ones whom you love most, to be accused wrongly, to have attributed to you mean and low motives that had never been a part of your thinking—things that had never for an instant entered your mind. And the accusations are not being made by a stranger, an enemy, but by a loved one, an individual who is more than a friend—one of the same flesh and blood. How does one react? In anger? No. In bitterness? No. In sorrow? Yes. But does one compromise with principle, with right, with truth? No. There is no compromise and never shall there be—not even when the companionship of one's own flesh and blood is at stake. A

---

[20]HC 2:294, 295, 297.

few days later, William wrote a letter acknowledging that he was in error and was too ashamed to see the Prophet in person. He asked Joseph Smith to forgive him, which the Prophet gladly did.

If Joseph Smith could have had loyalty and support from those who at one time or another professed to be his friends, how it could have changed things. An evil man in a high and holy calling can cause distress and destruction that an outsider could never cause. How much different the history of Joseph Smith would read if all had been loyal.

The Prophet Did Not Cease to Be a Man

Joseph Smith was what he was. Then why did some in the past and why do some people today try to make him something he was not? He was a great individual. Yet, many of his associates were not satisfied. They arbitrarily assigned perfection to him and then inwardly felt regret when they found weakness in Joseph and openly expressed disappointment because of that which Joseph yet lacked.

Prophets must be "sensitive"—sensitive to the Spirit of God, sensitive to the needs of their people, and sensitive to personal strengths and weaknesses.

Nephi lamented his inability to be as righteous as he thought he ought to be. He marveled over his weakness after that which he had beheld, and pleaded with God to help him to be better. Nephi honestly recognized his imperfections and wrote of them.[21] Moroni lamented his own inabilities and in essence prayed to God that his personal limitations would not be a "stumbling block" to the Gentiles. Yet God accepted their efforts as sufficient and put the responsibility on the Gentiles.[22] These prophets shared in common certain characteristics of all prophets—human imperfections and a desire to be better. So it was with the Prophet Joseph Smith.

Joseph Smith was a man who was called of God to be a prophet. When he received that call, he did not cease to be a

[21] 2 Nephi 4:16-35.
[22] Ether 12:23-29.

man. In essence, he humbly said of himself: "I am a rough stone. The sound of hammer and chisel were never heard on me until the Lord took me in hand."[23] He was near the end of his eventful life when he made this statement, and the hammer and chisel had been applied to him extensively prior to this time. Yet with all of the shaping and smoothing that had been done, he still saw himself as a "rough stone," but a rough stone in the process of becoming a polished shaft one day.

Joseph never hid his weaknesses. He permitted others to view them and ever wrote of them as had other prophets before him. Yet ever so many have considered it a remarkable discovery when they found weaknesses in the Prophet.

In spite of Joseph's candid evaluation of himself, there were those who rejected his description of what he was and wanted him to be something else, a perfect individual. From the days of Symonds Ryder, who apostatized because Joseph misspelled his last name, there have been those who have determined what Joseph ought to be and then reviled him because he was not what they had designated him to be. This continues today. There are those who feel that they have made a remarkable discovery when they find a weakness in the Prophet. Joseph Smith was what he was. He was a great Prophet and a great man. He was acknowledged as such by the Lord Jesus Christ, and by his faithful associates in the kingdom of God, and by many honest men outside the kingdom.

In fairness to Joseph Smith, we ought to view him as he was—partly polished, partly rough, the polished portion becoming ever more extensive. If we consider carefully the life of Joseph the Prophet, we cannot overlook the polishing process, and we can see the emerging of a great individual. If we view the life of Joseph Smith as a continual reducing of the rough areas and a continual enlarging of smooth areas, we shall not be disappointed in what we see, but will never cease to be astonished with the greatness of the man who was called of God.

---

[23]HC 5:401.

The excitement in studying the life of Joseph Smith is in seeing a dynamic, emerging Joseph in the process of becoming one who is responding to the touch of the hammer and chisel in the hand of God. Many view his life in this way and make applications as needed in their own lives so that they may also decrease the rough places and enlarge the smooth places.

A Lesson from History—Follow the Lord's Prophet

I suppose that if one were to lose the spirit of the Lord and begin to think of himself as superior to many of those who had been called to positions of prominence, it would be quite natural for such a person who had not been called to assume that the Prophet had fallen and was no longer in communication with God; otherwise he obviously would have received revelation to call "superior people." The "superior" person in his own way of thinking now has an obvious duty to work against the Prophet for the good of himself and other members of the Church. Hence, the apostate, lifted up in pride, seeing things from the viewpoint of his own egotism, might consider himself almost noble in opposing rather than supporting the Prophet. Such fatal errors can be avoided by following the humble example of our Lord and Savior Jesus Christ. Jesus on occasions made such statements as ". . . Why callest thou me good? There is none good but one, that is, God."[24] "O my Father, if it be possible, let this cup pass from me, nevertheless not as I will, but as thou wilt."[25] He also taught that unless we humble ourselves and become as a little child, we cannot enter the kingdom of heaven.[26] Jesus in his life always exemplified meekness and submissiveness to his Father.

Heber C. Kimball has given the following wise counsel:

I consider those trees in the forest which have the largest and highest tops are in the greatest danger: they are blown down; and there is no way of restoring them but to cut them off. Let the stump

[24]Mark 10:18.
[25]Matthew 26:39.
[26]Mark 10:13-15.

go back, and new sprouts come out. Those who have most responsibility are in most danger. We must be careful how we treat God's officers.[27]

He continued:

No man ever fell, unless it was through rejecting counsel. I as well as my brethren see this. My superior knows more than I, because he is nearer the fountain. To get knowledge, begin at the foot of the stream, and drink all up till you get to the fountain, and then you get all the knowledge.[28]

Elder Kimball was in a key position to view the consequences of disloyalty to the individual, to the Prophet, and to the Church: hence, he gave wise counsel and sounded a warning voice on many occasions. Following is another insightful quotation from him:

I will give you a key which Brother Joseph Smith used to give in Nauvoo. He said, that the very step of apostasy commenced with losing confidence in the leaders of this Church and Kingdom, and that whenever you discerned that spirit, you might know that it would lead the possessor of it on the road to apostasy. If then you have got this spirit in your hearts, . . . I say, there is the spirit of apostasy, there is a place where the Spirit of God does not abide in its fulness.

It is for us to learn to be obedient in our callings and to the Priesthood, in our several quorums and families, and in all circles where we associate together. This is a lesson which must be learned, and when you learn the doctrine of obedience, you will have power to control the weaknesses of your nature, to control yourselves in every respect. But you never will learn this lesson, and gain this knowledge, until you are willing to be controlled by those who lead you in this kingdom.[29]

On this same subject a modern day apostle and a member of the First Presidency, Harold B. Lee, says:

I remember the prophetic pronouncement that was made from this stand by President George Albert Smith eighteen months ago when he said:

. . . Many have belittled Joseph Smith, and those who have will be forgotten in the remains of mother earth and their infamy will be ever with them, but honor, majesty, and fidelity to God attached to Joseph Smith's name and exmplified by him will never die.

[27]HC 6:30.
[28]*Ibid.*
[29]JD 3:270-71.

I wish that statement could be heard to all ends of the earth.

I want to bear you my testimony that the experience I have had has taught me that those who criticize the leaders of this church are showing signs of a spiritual sickness, which unless curbed, will bring about eventually spiritual death. I want to bear my testimony as well as those who in public seek by their criticism, to belittle our leaders or bring them into disrepute, will bring upon themselves more hurt than upon those whom they seek thus to malign. I have watched over the years, and I have read of the history of many of those who fell away from this Church and I want to bear testimony that no apostate who ever left the Church ever prospered as an influence in his community thereafter.[30]

The Future Can Be Different

As I review the events in the history of the Church and particularly in the life of Joseph Smith, I find myself asking the question, "What if?" What if Oliver Cowdery had not apostatized? What if the people had not speculated wildly in Kirtland? What if Colonel Hinckle had not betrayed Joseph Smith at Far West? What if Joseph Smith could have had greater loyalty? What if. . .?

Sometimes as I reflect upon events in quiet moments, my mind goes beyond just asking "What if. . .?" Something within protests, and I cry out mentally: STOP! Let's rerun that scene again; let's try it a different way. Let's have the events just the same, but this time, let's have all give their loyalty to the Prophet Joseph Smith and then let's view the outcome. But there is no way to rerun a historical incident. The scene has been played out, and the Prophet is dead. No, the scene cannot be changed, but it is obvious that the lessons of history should not be overlooked nor disregarded. The price of disloyalty to all parties concerned is tragically high. We are still a people led by a prophet. We are still a people faced with perils. Will our faith be greater? Will we be more trustworthy? Will the prophet of today and tomorrow have our loyal support? Or will dissenting, hurtful voices be raised and harmful acts be repeated? The past cannot be altered, but the future can be different.

[30]CR, October 1947, pp. 66-67.

7 THE PROPHET JOSEPH IN ETERNAL PERSPECTIVE

Joseph Smith—the Lord's Prophet

Some see Joseph as one thing and others see him as another. It would seem that what a person sees Joseph Smith as being may partly be determined by what the individual himself is. If men in varying degrees of imperfection have a difficult time knowing what Joseph Smith is really like, then it might be wise to consider the evaluation of one who has no imperfections and by his own admission has all knowledge. It is apparent by just a casual perusal of the scriptures that our Lord and Savior Jesus Christ sees Joseph Smith as a worthy servant and a worthy prophet. He visited him more than once. He communicated with him, inspired him, and comforted him on almost innumerable occasions.

He restored the priesthood and the gospel through him. Heavenly messengers by the score visited him. He was worthy enough to have all this happen to him. What he was, was sufficient to perform the greatest mission for the Lord Jesus Christ ever performed by a man. Joseph Smith was permitted to see the Savior on more than one occasion. In addition to the glorious First Vision, when Jesus Christ with God the Father visited Joseph, He also appeared in the Kirtland Temple. The building had been built at great sacrifice. After the dedication, Joseph and Oliver prayed, and there appeared the Son of God. Joseph's beautiful description of the event follows:

The veil was taken from our minds, and the eyes of our understanding were opened.

We saw the Lord standing upon the breastwork of the pulpit, before us; and under his feet was a paved work of pure gold, in color like amber.

His eyes were as a flame of fire; the hair of his head was white like the pure snow; his contenance shone above the brightness of the sun; and his voice was as the sound of the rushing of great waters, even the voice of Jehovah, saying:

I am the first and the last; I am he who liveth, I am he who was slain; I am your advocate with the Father.[1]

Joseph, in company with Sidney Rigdon in 1832, beheld a most glorious vision. They saw the glory of God, His kingdom, the fate of the righteous and the wicked; and they saw the Lord Jesus Christ and bore this following testimony:

And we beheld the glory of the Son, on the right hand of the Father, and received of his fulness;

And saw the holy angels, and them who are sanctified before his throne, worshipping God, and the Lamb, who worship him forever and ever.

And now, after the many testimonies which have been given of him, this is the testimony, last of all, which we give of him: That he lives!

For we saw him, even on the right hand of God; and we heard the voice bearing record that he is the Only Begotten of the Father. . . .[2]

Vision After Vision

In addition to personal visitations, our Lord sent numerous heavenly beings, holy angels, to instruct Joseph and to bestow keys of authority upon him. Foremost among these in terms of frequency of appearance was Moroni, who had a very special relationship with Joseph. He was the Prophet's tutor. By appointment, once each year, Joseph Smith met with Moroni to be instructed. Orson Pratt wrote:

. . . for the space of four years; during which, whenever Joseph needed chastisement he received it at the appointed time; his

---

[1]D&C 110:1-4.
[2]D&C 76:20-23.

failings were corrected; he was shown whenever he erred; and he was taught what to do: he was instructed, little by little, until he learned, by practice to do the will of God.[3]

The Prophet's mother, Lucy Mack Smith, also informs us about her son's intimate relationship with his heavenly teacher. She also indicates that there were occasions when the angel had cause to rebuke her young son.

Presently he [Joseph] smiled and said, 'I have taken the severest chastisement that I have ever had in my life.'

My husband, supposing that it was from some of the neighbors, was quite angry and observed, 'I would like to know what business anybody has to find fault with you!'

'Stop, father, stop,' said Joseph, 'it was the angel of the Lord. As I passed by the hill of Cumorah, where the plates are, the angel met me and said that I had not been engaged enough in the work of the Lord; that the time had come for the record to be brought forth; and that I must be up and doing and set myself about the things which God had commanded me to do. But, father, give yourself no uneasiness concerning the reprimand which I have received, for I now know the course that I am to pursue, so all will be well.[4]

The Prophet's mother also gives some insight concerning the great amount of knowledge Joseph received during the four-year period of preparation:

During our evening conversations, Joseph would occasionally give us some of the most amusing recitals that could be imagined. He would describe the ancient inhabitants of this continent, their dress, mode of traveling, and the animals upon which they rode; their mode of warfare; and also their religious worship. This he would do with as much ease, seemingly, as if he had spent his whole life among them.[5]

In 1829 Joseph and Oliver knelt and asked God about baptism, and there appeared John the Baptist. He had died as a martyr while on the earth. He was beheaded, but he stood before them as a perfect, glorious, resurrected being and bestowed upon them the Aaronic Priesthood. Oliver says of this occasion:

[3]JD 19:15.
[4]HJS 100-101.
[5]Ibid., p. 83.

. . . . the veil was parted and the angel of God came down clothed with glory, and delivered the anxiously looked for message. . . . His voice, though mild, pierced to the center, and his words, 'I am thy fellow servant' dispelled every fear. We listened, we gazed, we admired! 'Twas the voice of an angel, from glory, 'twas a message from the Most High! And as we heard we rejoiced, while his love enkindled upon our souls, and we were wrapped in the vision of the Almighty.[6]

A few weeks later, the three chief apostles of Jesus Christ—Peter, James, and John—came to the earth and gave Joseph and Oliver the higher priesthood—the Holy Priesthood after the Order of the Son of God, or Melchezedik Priesthood. Moses, Elijah, and Elias also appeared and bestowed keys upon the young prophet. John Taylor, a close associate of Joseph's, said that there were additional heavenly messengers:

I know of what I speak, for I was very well acquainted with him and was with him a great deal during his life and was with him when he died.

The principles which he had placed him in communication with the Lord, and not only with the Lord, but with the ancient apostles and prophets; such men, for instance, as Abraham, Isaac, Jacob, Noah, Adam, Seth, Enoch, and Jesus and the Father, and the apostles that lived on this continent as well as those who lived on the Asiatic continent. *He seemed to be as familiar with these people as we are with one another.* Why? Because he had to introduce a dispensation which was called the dispensation of the fulness of times. . . .[7] (Italics added.)

John Taylor on another occasion said:

And when Joseph Smith was raised up as a Prophet of God, *Mormon, Moroni, Nephi, and others* of the ancient prophets who formerly lived on this continent, and Peter and John and others who lived on the Asiatic Continent, came to him and communicated to him certain principles pertaining to the Gospel of the Son of God.[8] (Italics added.)

George Q. Cannon adds:

He [Joseph Smith] was visited constantly by angels. . . . *Moroni,* in the beginning as you know, to prepare him for his mission came

[6]Pearl of Great Price, p. 57, footnote.
[7]JD 21:94.
[8]*Ibid.*, 17:374.

and ministered and talked to him from time to time, *and he had vision after vision* in order that his mind might be fully saturated with knowledge of the things of God, and that he might comprehend the great and holy calling that God has bestowed upon him.[9] (Italics added.)

On another occasion, John Taylor told further of Joseph's greatness:

. . . the spirit of revelation rested down upon God's servant Joseph in these early days, who like Adam, Moses, Abraham, Jesus, Jared, Nephi, Moroni and others, had the heavens unfolded to his view, and although the Church was so few in number the principles and purposes of God were developed fully to the vision of his mind, and he gazed upon the things that are to transpire in the latter-days associated with the dispensation that he was called upon by the Almighty to introduce. He learned by communication from the heavens, from time to time, of the great events that should transpire in the latter days. He understood things that were past, and comprehended the various dispensations and designs of those dispensations. He not only had the principles developed, but he was conversant with the parties who officiated as the leading men of those dispensations, and from a number of them he received authority and keys and priesthood and power for the carrying out of the great purposes of the Lord in the last days, who were sent and commissioned specially by the Almighty to confer upon him those keys and this authority, and hence he introduced what was spoken of by all the prophets since the world was; the dispensation in which we live, which differs from all other dispensations in that it is the dispensation of the fulness of times, embracing all other dispensations, all other powers, all other keys and all other privileges and immunities that ever existed upon the face of the earth . . . which was altogether ahead of all the intelligence that existed in the world.[10]

Let us just pause and think for a moment what it would mean to a mortal on this earth to see and hear, be instructed by, and receive authority from many of God's greatest prophets. Such knowledge and wisdom would be almost beyond comprehension—not just because they had lived on the earth at various times and were among the greatest men who ever lived, but also because they came immediately from the presence of God to Joseph Smith. What a way to be educated—personal

[9]*Ibid.*, 23:362.
[10]*Ibid.*, 20:174-75.

visitations and visions of the eternal world! Little wonder that Joseph's followers said of him:

I have sometimes thought that the Prophet Joseph, with the knowledge he possessed and the progress he had made could not stay with the people, so slow were we to comprehend things and so enshrouded in our ignorant traditions. The Saints could not comprehend Joseph Smith; the Elders could not; the Apostles could not. They did so a little towards the close of his life, but his knowledge was so extensive and his comprehension so great that they could not rise to it.[11] (George Q. Cannon)

Brother Joseph used a great many methods of testing the integrity of men; and he taught a great many things which, in consequence of tradition, required prayer, faith, and a testimony from the Lord, before they could be believed by many of the Saints. His mind was opened by the visions of the Almighty, and the Lord taught him many things by vision and revelation that were never taught publicly in his days; for the people could not bear the flood of intelligence which God poured into his mind.[12] (Wilford Woodruff)

Joseph Smith Was Foreordained

The Lord saw Joseph Smith in eternal perspective. He saw him as one chosen to perform a great mission on the earth. Thousands of years prior to his actual birth on the earth, Joseph who was sold into Egypt knew this and prophesied of it. A prophet who lived on the earth during and after the life of Joseph Smith spoke of it. John Taylor spoke of the fore-ordination of the prophet of the last dispensation as follows:

We all look upon Joseph Smith as being a Prophet of God. God called him to occupy the position that he did. How long ago? Thousands of years ago before this world was formed. The prophets prophesied about his coming. . . .[13]

President John Taylor further declared:

Joseph Smith in the first place was set apart by the Almighty according to the counsels of the Gods in the eternal worlds, to introduce the principles of life among the people of which the Gospel is the grand power and influence, and through which salvation can extend to all peoples, all nations, all kindreds, all tongues, and all

---

[11]*Millennial Star*, 61:629.
[12]JD 5:83-84.
[13]JD 26:106.

worlds. It is the principle that brings life and immortality to light, and places us in communication with God. God selected him for that purpose, and he fulfilled his mission and lived honorably and died honorably.[14]

When the foreordained Prophet Joseph Smith came to earth, the Lord had enough confidence in his integrity to bestow all of the keys of the priesthood upon him. What an awesome responsibility for a man! Few who have ever lived have been so honored. The Lord trusted him enough to put into his young and inexperienced hands a priceless book of scripture, the continued existence of which had great eternal importance. It had been prepared hundreds of years before by the most competent and inspired men on the earth and had been carefully safeguarded for centuries to come forth in the latter days to bring the peoples of the earth to the fulness of the gospel; and it was entrusted to the Lord's servant Joseph. He also called his servant Joseph to prepare a book of scripture, the Doctrine and Covenants—a book almost entirely written by Joseph's own hand, a book of revelations from his God. The book has come to occupy a distinctive place as a companion book of scripture to the Bible and the Book of Mormon. In addition, a fourth book of scripture, the Pearl of Great Price, a compilation of the works of Joseph Smith has been published since his death. As one reads the scriptures, one is left with the distinct impression that the Lord had complete confidence in Joseph Smith; and of all those on the earth, it was his servant Joseph, and only his servant Joseph, whom he so trusted. There have been but few in the past who have enjoyed as much of the confidence, and hence the power, of God.

Testimonies of Joseph's Associates

As a servant of the all-powerful Eternal God, Joseph Smith did not have to depend upon the witnesses nor the praise of men to establish himself as a prophet. His master was God, and God poured out his spirit on those who were faithful and

---

[14]Burton, Alma P., *Discourses of the Prophet Joseph Smith* (Salt Lake City: Deseret Book Co.), p. 16.

obedient, and they bore testimony that Joseph truly was called of God and directed by him.

Heber C. Kimball bore his witness as follows:

. . . You will not doubt in relation to the truth of what the world calls "Mormonism," for the Church of Jesus Christ of Latter-day Saints, established and organized through the instrumentality of the Prophet Joseph Smith, is the true Church of God. With it is the Priesthood and power of God; and you might as well try to doubt that the sun shines, for it is truth; and although all hell may deny it, and all the men upon the earth, that will make no difference, for it is from God. The Lord called that man, and sent his angels to ordain him and confer upon him that authority necessary for the building up of the Kingdom of God; and it was through him that we received all the authority we hold, and through us every soul of you who have received the truth received it—through that Priesthood which came from God through Joseph Smith. . . .[15]

Wilford Woodruff said of Joseph Smith:

It has been my faith and belief from the time that I was made acquainted with the gospel that no greater prophet than Joseph Smith ever lived on the face of the earth save Jesus Christ. He was raised up to stand at the head of this great dispensation—the greatest of all dispensations God has ever given to man.[16]

Wilford Woodruff bore the following testimony of Joseph Smith:

The mind of the Prophet was opened by the spirit of revelation, so that he could see and comprehend a great deal; but he required the Spirit of the living God—the inspiration of the Almighty to rest upon him continually, to qualify him for the great duties that were constantly increasing upon him. . . .[17]

John Taylor said of the first prophet of this dispensation:

He was the representative of God, his credentials came from God, and his mission extended not to one nation only, but to all nations; and he was authorized to establish and organize what was termed the Church and Kingdom of God upon the earth. And every step that he took, every principle that he inculcated, and every doctrine that he taught, came from God by the revelations of God to him, and through him to the people.[18]

---

[15]JD 8:248-49.
[16]*Ibid.*, 21:317.
[17]*Ibid.*, 7:99.
[18]*Ibid.*, 19:303.

President Taylor, speaking on another occasion, said:

. . . I believe that Joseph Smith revealed more in relation to the Kingdom of God, and was a greater Prophet than perhaps any other man who ever lived except Jesus Christ.[19]

Brigham Young spoke as follows:

There are a goodly number in the congregation, who have been acquainted with this Church and Kingdom from its rise, and . . . they knew Joseph—they knew him week to week, and from year to year, they knew what he did, they knew how he spake, they knew the spirit he possessed, they were acquainted with it, it is the same spirit they possess to the present day—the spirit of "Mormonism," the spirit of the Gospel. I will ask those brethren, and those sisters, if they believe Joseph Smith was a Prophet of God? If they believe that he magnified his calling? I will ask them if Joseph lived and died a Prophet of God, and what would they answer? All men and women know by the power of the Holy Ghost, by the spirit they know it. . . .[20]

Joseph F. Smith said tens of thousands knew Joseph Smith was a prophet of God:

Consequently, as I have said, Joseph Smith is held in reverence, his name is honored; tens of thousands of people thank God in their heart and from the depths of their souls for the knowledge the Lord has restored to the earth through him, and therefore they speak well of him and bear testimony of his worth. . . .

They speak to his praise, to his honor, and they hold his name in honorable remembrance. They revere him and they love him as they love no other man, because they know he was the chosen instrument in the hands of the Almighty of restoring the Gospel of life and salvation unto them.[21]

Joseph Smith, an Extraordinary Servant

All men have free agency, and to communicate with or receive blessings from God, one has to fulfill the law upon which the blessings are predicated. To have had the experiences that he had, Joseph Smith had to be a remarkably righteous person, an unusually humble and devoted servant. To suggest that Joseph Smith was not a completely worthy individual would be

---

[19]*Ibid.*, 17:47.
[20]*Ibid.*, 1:81-82.
[21]*Ibid.*, 24:9.

to deny the very most basic truths of the gospel of Jesus Christ.

After the death of "His Servant Joseph," the Lord caused to have written and included as scripture the following, so that it becomes the Lord's statement:

> To seal the testimony of this book and the Book of Mormon, we announce the martyrdom of Joseph Smith the Prophet. . . . *Joseph Smith, the Prophet and Seer of the Lord, has done more, save Jesus only, for the salvation of men in this world, than another other man that ever lived in it.* In the short space of twenty years, he has brought forth the Book of Mormon, which he translated by the gift and power of God, and has been the means of publishing it on two continents; has sent the fulness of the everlasting gospel, which it contained, to the four quarters of the earth; has brought forth the revelations and commandments which compose this book of Doctrine and Covenants, and many other wise documents and instructions for the benefit of the children of men; gathered many thousands of the Latter-day Saints, founded a great city, and left a fame and name that cannot be slain. He lived great, and he died great in the eyes of God and his people; and like most of the Lord's anointed in ancient times, has sealed his mission and his works with his own blood.[22] (Italics added.)

"Save Jesus only, Joseph the Prophet has done more for the salvation of man in the world than any other." As one reads this and other scriptures, one is left with no doubt of God's confidence in Joseph Smith. Joseph had a remarkably intimate relationship with God—a relationship which can only be established upon the basis of some well-defined eternal principles. To associate with God, one must have unwavering faith in him and must be willing to forsake his sins and subject his own will to the will of God. The acceptance of Joseph Smith by the Lord is an irrefutable witness of Joseph Smith's personal qualities. The Lord has said that "the powers of heaven cannot be controlled nor handled only upon the principles of righteousness."[23]

There are those who have said, and still say, that it is difficult to know what Joseph Smith was really like. It seems that God knew. From God's perfect point of view, Joseph Smith

---

[22]D&C 135:1, 3.
[23]D&C 121:36.

was an extraordinary servant and one whom He trusted implicitly. There are many ways of viewing Joseph Smith, but apparently from the Lord's vantage point, there were few who ever lived upon the earth who could compare with his servant Joseph. The Lord had unlimited confidence in Joseph Smith, and those who knew and served the same God that Joseph knew bore strong witness that he was God's servant and that God loved him and sustained him. This should be an indication to us that we may also safely put our confidence in Joseph Smith as a prophet of the living God, and we need not fear that we will be disappointed. He did not disappoint God, and he will not disappoint us. Man's vision and knowledge is limited, but God's is not.

Joseph Smith, Head of Our Dispensation

Joseph Smith was being prepared in this life by the Lord for a contribution in the next life. He was to occupy a very important role eternally, and to occupy that role well he had to have certain experiences here on earth. That does not mean that God brought the heartache, the suffering, the brutality into Joseph Smith's life. God is not the author of evil, but of good. He is not the author of unhappiness, but of happiness. It does mean, however, that men exercised their free agency and brought misery into the life of Joseph; and the Lord did not immediately change that condition but let Joseph Smith the prophet learn from it.

It appears as we read the account of Joseph's life, that an unusual amount of adversity was crowded into his thirty-eight years. His life was not long, but it was literally filled with situations that were hard to bear. The Lord told him during his painful confinement at Liberty, ". . . Know thou, my son, that all these things shall give thee experience, and shall be for thy good."[24]

It has been the practice of our Father in heaven to call one person to stand at the head of a dispensation; and that one

---

[24]D&C 122:7.

person, a prophet of the living God, was blessed and received from God an unusual outpouring of heavenly things. That prophet then became the chief witness to the people of that dispensation that God in reality lives and that his gospel is on the earth. The testimony of the prophet then became the way to God and to His blessings. Those who accept the prophet as a true prophet come to God, and those who reject him cannot come to God.

Joseph Smith holds this unique and responsible position in the last dispensation. He will always stand at the head of the dispensation of the fulness of times. This is testified of by succeeding prophets. President Brigham Young said:

> Permit me, my hearers, brethren and strangers, to say to you, there is not that man that hears the sound of my voice this day, that can say that Jesus lives, whether he professes to be his disciple or not; and can say at the same time, that Joseph Smith was not a Prophet of the Lord. . . . Jesus lives, and is the Savior of the world, Joseph Smith is a Prophet of God, and lives in the bosom of his father Abraham. Though they have killed his body, yet he lives and beholds the face of his Father in Heaven; and his garments are pure as the angels that surround the throne of God; and no man on the earth can say that Jesus lives, and deny at the same time my assertion about the Prophet Joseph. This is my testimony, and it is strong.[25]

Brigham Young further says:

> He [*Joseph Smith*] *is at home, and still holds the keys of the Kingdom, which were committed to him by heavenly messengers, and always will.* Do you ask who brother Brigham is? He is a humble instrument in the hands of God, to keep His people in the path which He has marked out through the instrumentality of His servant Joseph; and to travel in which is all I ask of them. . . . Thus the Lord found him, and called him to be a Prophet, and made him a successful instrument in laying the foundation of His kingdom . . . and to whom the Lord gave the keys of this last dispensation, which were not to be taken from him in time, neither will they be in eternity.
>
> I wish to see this people fulfill in every particular what Joseph told them to do, and build up the Kingdom of God, and this they are doing.[26] (Italics added.)

---

[25]JD, 1:38.
[26]*Ibid.*, 2:127.

This is verified by George Q. Cannon:

He [Joseph] stands at the head. He is a unique character, differing from every other man in this respect, and excelling every other man. Because he was the head, God chose him, and while he was faithful no man could take his place and position. He was faithful, and died faithful. He stands therefore at the head of this dispensation, and will throughout all eternity, and no man can take that power away from him. If any man holds these keys, he holds them subordinate to him. You never heard President Young teach any other doctrine; he always said that Joseph stood at the head of this dispensation; that Joseph holds the keys; that although Joseph had gone behind the veil he stood at the head of this dispensation, and that he himself held the keys subordinate to him. President Taylor teaches the same doctrine, and you will never hear any other doctrine from any of the faithful Apostles or servants of God, who understand the order of the Holy Priesthood. If we get our salvation we shall have to pass by him; if we enter into our glory it will be through the authority that he has received. We cannot get around him. . . .[27]

Additional insight to Joseph Smith's eternal role is given by President Young:

Joseph Smith holds the keys of this last dispensation, and is now engaged behind the veil in the great work of the last days. . . . No man or woman in this dispensation will ever enter into the Celestial Kingdom of God without the consent of Joseph Smith. I cannot go there without his consent. He holds the keys of that kingdom for the last dispensation. Should not this comfort all people? They will, by and by, be a thousand times more thankful for such a man as Joseph Smith, Junior, than it is possible for them to be for any earthly good whatever. It is his mission to see that all the children of men in this last dispensation are saved, that can be, through the redemption. You will be thankful, every one of you, that Joseph Smith, Junior was ordained to this great calling before the worlds were.[28]

The continuing active role of Joseph Smith in the eternal world is further attested to.

In 1856, President Jedediah M. Grant, a counselor to President Brigham Young, during a serious illness was permitted

[27]Ibid., 23:361.
[28]Ibid., 7:289.

to visit the spirit world and reported what he had seen and heard to Heber C. Kimball, also a counselor in the First Presidency of the Church. Among other things, he reported a conversation with his deceased wife Caroline, who had died on the plains. President Kimball, referring to Jedediah M. Grant's experience, said:

> He asked his wife Caroline where Joseph and Hyrum and Father Smith and others were; she replied, "They have gone away ahead, to perform and transact business for us. The same as when Brother Brigham and his brethren left Winter Quarters came here to search out a home; they came to find a location for their brethren."[29]

Often we hear, "Why did he or why did she have to suffer so? Why did he or she have to die?" The answers are not readily available; but when this question is raised concerning the first prophet of the last dispensation, a partial answer at least can be given because of the information revealed concerning Joseph Smith in the perspective of eternity. It would seem that as great as Joseph's mission was on the earth, it was just a preview of, an introduction to, his mission in eternity. The Lord was concerned not just with the development of a prophet-leader for this life, but with the development of an eternal prophet-leader. Joseph had a vast responsibility on the earth, but that responsibility has expanded in the eternal world. The answers to all the "why" questions asked by Joseph and his followers were not available in earth life, but most assuredly those answers are known in the perspective of eternity. The Lord's way of developing an eternal servant and leader will always be hard to comprehend in this life. Joseph Smith had the faith in his Lord Jesus Christ to believe that this life and its experiences had purpose in the wisdom of God; and he was willing, even in death, to make God's will his will.

If one did not have the perspective of eternity, if one did not know that Joseph Smith is to be forever a great leader of those born in the last dispensation, one would tend to over-emphasize the tragedy of a life of harassment and an untimely violent death.

---

[29]*Ibid.*, 4:136.

Joseph's birth was known and recorded nearly four thousand years before he was born. It is remarkable that Joseph who was sold into Egypt was able to see ahead thousands of years to our day. He envisioned a latter-day prophet, a "choice seer" who would be raised up and would do a great work among the ancient Joseph's decendents. The Hebrew who had been sold into bondage and had distinguished the name Joseph through his circumspect behavior and his noble deeds prophesied that the latter-day prophet whom he envisioned would also be named Joseph. Further insight into the greatness of the latter-day prophet is also given because Joseph who was sold into Egypt recorded, "and he shall be like unto me."[30] What a remarkable prophecy nearly four thousand years before the birth of Joseph Smith! His birth was known, as well as his greatness. What a compliment to Joseph Smith to be named after and compared to the noble Joseph who was sold into Egypt! Also, what a compliment for Joseph who was sold into Egypt to be compared to the Joseph of the last dispensation. Joseph Smith occupies a position unique among prophets.

He was the designated head of a dispensation of the gospel. This in itself puts him in a small and very select group of prophets. Further, Joseph Smith was chosen to head the last dispensation—the dispensation of the fulness of times—the dispensation of the gospel in which all things would be restored—the dispensation when all things would be gathered together into one—the dispensation which would prepare for the return of Jesus Christ to the earth and the ushering in of the millennial reign.

As the head of this dispensation, Joseph was the instrument in the Lord's hands through which authority and gospel principles were restored to the earth for the last time. He also stands at the head of this dispensation, and all who live during this dispensation of the gospel are subject to him.

---

[30]2 Nephi 3:15.

Joseph Smith, a Continuing Example

Joseph Smith has continued in his eternal progression and is no longer with us on this earth. But his example lives on in the lives of countless Latter-day Saints, self-sacrificing, honest, dedicated Latter-day Saints who say with their actions as Joseph said with his, "Thy will be done."

Those who lived contemporary with Joseph Smith had the advantage of knowing him personally. But we who live well over a century since he was on the earth are not without advantages. We have an advantage of perspective that those who lived with him did not have. We have the privilege of viewing Joseph Smith by the perspective of time. We can, if we desire, focus very closely through the eyes of those who knew him, or we can move back to a vantage point of a great distance and view him on a stage of great width and depth.

Continually one's horizons are expanded with regard to the greatness of the contribution that Joseph Smith made and also the greatness of the man himself. Time has a way of supporting the truly great and exposing those who would feign greatness.

The Lord called Joseph not just to be an example and guide to those of his own day, those who had the opportunity of knowing him personally. His greatness, and the greatness of his teachings, were to benefit those who would come after. Joseph Smith can belong to us today just as he did to his associates in former days.

In days past, individuals had to extend themselves to hear Joseph, to know him, and to understand him. Today this is still the case. One must extend himself to know Joseph Smith. His writings and his many teachings are now readily available, but it requires effort to seek, to probe, to know. But after the effort is extended, one is never the same again. To know the Prophet is to know true greatness. To know Joseph is to feel an influence that has persisted with the passing years. The influence of Joseph Smith, sustained by God, has always persuaded men to be better, to reach higher, to overcome the world, and to live nearer to God.

As one travels through the Church today, one is impressed with an obvious dynamic witness that Joseph Smith was what he said he was, that he was acting for and in the name of the Lord Jesus Christ.

Joseph Smith established God's Church on the earth; and the Church as it expands, grows, and develops worthy people throughout the world, is a testimony and an irrefutable witness that Joseph Smith was a prophet. Joseph Smith does not belong to the past alone but to the present and to the future. Each new generation of Latter-day Saints, whether children of members or converts, will feel great joy as they become acquainted with Joseph Smith. They will gain courage through Joseph's example. They will gain insights into life and eternity.

Joseph Smith Is What He Said He Was

My quest began with the question "What manner of man was this Joseph Smith?" I have not yet gained the total answer, but I have gained some insight into the nature of the prophet of the restoration. I have learned enough at this point in my continuing quest to witness that he was in every deed what he said he was. Joseph Smith is a prophet of God. I have become somewhat familiar with his life, and have sought to serve the same God that he served, and have sought to live the gospel he restored. If one did less than this, I do not see how he would come to know that God's prophet was in reality God's prophet. Because intellect—as vital, necessary and important as it is—is not enough. Application of true principles in one's own life and the reception of the Holy Spirit in one's own soul are necessary prerequisites to understanding and conviction. Such conviction comes gradually. It comes line upon line, precept upon precept, with learning and application, repentance and re-application. The whisperings of the Spirit become unmistakable. As one experience follows another, there is a consistant commonalty in spiritual experiences. Belief gives way to knowledge, and conviction becomes immovable as witness after witness follows experience after experience. And the mind is enlightened and the soul enlarged. And in the scheme of things, the life and mission of Joseph Smith looms larger and larger, and one is filled with gratitude for his life and for one's knowledge of him.

Truly he is what he claimed to be—a prophet of God. No prophet of God is ordinary, but among extraordinary prophets, Joseph is unique and distinctive. The latter-day scriptures bear witness that save Jesus Christ only Joseph Smith did more for the salvation of men in this world than any one else. That is scripture, and it is true. Why is it scripture? Why is it true? Because with the exception of Jesus Christ, Joseph Smith had the most important assignment upon this earth. Jesus Christ, of course, is incomparable. He was a member of the Godhead before he came to this earth, he was divine on this earth, and he was resurrected to take his place at the right hand of his Father.

Joseph Smith was a man—a distant second, but second, which places him in a remarkable position. In the pre-existent life he was chosen to be the head of the dispensation of the fulness of times.

As he came to earth he had a great opportunity, and he fulfilled his assignment in an excellent manner. With all of his greatness before, during, and after his earth life, how humble was his behavior—so humble that there were many who rejected him as a prophet and rejected his eternal, life-giving teachings.

It had happened before in the lives of Noah, Jeremiah, Peter, and even the Lord Jesus Christ; and it will happen again because in a world of pretense, one devoid of it is often counted as naught except by those who have "a broken heart and contrite spirit," those who discern not only by the "natural" but also by the "spiritual." Those who lived during the life of Joseph, who applied the words of the Savior as the Prophet espoused them, came to know him as a representative of the Lord and followed him as a true prophet. Those who have lived after and followed the same pattern have also come to know, and their combined testimonies bear witness of him. I suggest they are true and valid witnesses.

May I also invite you to continue your own quest and more fully learn the answer to the query, "What manner of man was this Joseph Smith?"

INDEX